The Black Woman's Gumbo Ya-Ya

Quotations by Black Women
Edited by Terri L. Jewell

The Crossing Press, Freedom, CA 95019

Cover art by Jesse Sweetwater
Cover and book design by Sheryl Karas
Back cover photo by René Dawson

Printed in the U.S.A.

Library of Congress Cataloging-in-Publication Data

The Black woman's gumbo ya-ya : quotations by black women / edited
    by Terri L. Jewell.
                p. cm.
ISBN 0-89594-580-0 (cloth). -- ISBN 0-89594-579-7 (paper)
1. Afro-American women --Quotations. 2. Women, Black--Quotations.
I. Jewell, Terri L.
E185.86.B5415   1993
082'.08996--dc20
                                    93-11482
                                     CIP

Table of Contents

"gumbo ya-ya"
an introduction by hattie gossett

with "gumbo ya-ya" terri jewell provides black wimmins—& those who can learn from us—a tool for our life journey survival kits. what a tool. girlfriend worked! okay? this book mirrors our brilliance strengths dreams fears battles sorrows joys fun. it helps us put institutions & people who be trying to dis us & work our nerves in their place. it helps us say i love you to others & ourselves. in our own worldwide words!

anybody who needs to make words work for them can find help in "gumbo ya-ya." need to greet a friend give sensitive advice a speech a workshop? need to write a thank you note love letter term paper novel business report scientific extract? its all here. this book comes out of the global experiences of black wimmins who have pushed through miles & miles of isms. yet it speaks far beyond those limiting perimeters to the human need to do what we black folks call testifin—naming the realities of life.

carry this book in your backpack pocketbook briefcase backpocket or limousine so you can read bits & pieces while on your way to school work the clinic courthouse unemployment office welfare office—or during a business trip extended world cruise family visit pilgrimage. it can help you get ready for coming out or getting married. it can help you through that funeral christening retirement party big date. keep it on your desk by your easy chair or bedside in your kitchen or bathroom.

I wish "gumbo ya-ya" had been available during my childhood. when i grew up in the projects in a central jersey factorytown during the 1940s & 50s before most people of color could afford a telephone or television—there were no videos answering machines home computers fax machines in those days—people (gasp!) talked to each other. conversation was an everyday high art. we also read a lot. during conversation people often quoted from favorite books or simply from the latest book they had read. many people could endlessly quote long passages on almost any subject. plus we quoted folk tales & wise funny contrary things grandmama lula or uncle bigman said. these werent just intellectual people doing this reading & quoting. i am talking about everyday ordinary people.

community life centered mostly around the church. there were endless church programs for which children & adults had to memorize & recite epigrams monologues speeches poems by historical or literary figures—often white—almost always male. the bible & shakespeare were favorite source materials. so were those compendiums of quotes for all occasions. these programs were presented for christmas easter mothers day fathers day etc. plus there were occasions we observed that i dont hear about now—childrens day emancipation proclamation day homecoming day tom thumb wedding day etc. a book like "gumbo ya-ya" would have been truly appreciated. though we didnt know about black feminism we knew the power of wimmins words especially black wimmins words.

now we stand at the post-cold war crossroads looking for the sweetness of life in these pre-21st century days. now i belong to a global community which has new programs ceremonies occasions rituals to suit the way we live now. this book is right on time for people like me—& for todays church people too.

best of all this book can give us the last word. everybody knows the feeling of being in a situation that calls for a well-honed verbal too-shay which doesnt usually present itself during the heat or chill of the moment. with modern conveniences like the phone fax computer tape recorder overnight mail & "gumbo ya-ya" we can voice thoughts which only surface after the fact so we can then take ourselves on to the next moment. thank you diva terri for helping all of us with our homework for many years to come.

Introduction by Terri Jewell

This collection was born out of my personal need for affirmation as a Black woman. I needed a coping mechanism for the growing conservatism in this nation; during the Rodney King incident and rebellions afterwards; and upon hearing Sojourner Truth's "Ain't I A Woman" just one time too often—as if she were the only Black woman from the past whose words were worth repeating. I knew there were more than ten "quotable" Black women in the world and I challenged myself to find them. There are approximately 350 Black women from all over the world here.

"Gumbo Ya-Ya" means "rich words, found words." The term "gumbo" means not only a savory soup, but is derived from a Bantu word, "ngombo." This means "the real word." "Gumbo" may also have connections to the Zulu word "ngcono" which means "improved, better, recovered." The term "ya-ya" among Australian aborigine becomes "yabber" (pronounced "yabba") which means "the word spoken." "Gumbo Ya-Ya," then, are the thoughts, observ-ations, viewpoints, the songs, poetry and dreams of Black women *about* and *for* Black women. By and large, I took excerpts from nonfiction and poetry only—no fiction. And since proverbs (usually accepted as poetry) are created out of the experiences of individuals and their communities, I included those affirmative ones about Black women. Whenever possible, I included the original cultural rendering since black languages, too, are negated in this country.

Here are Black women's words you can use. Fold one tiny and put it into a sacred place close to you. Place them in personal letters and lectures, over your desk at work and among your prayers. Give them to your enemies, stitch them into blankets, sip them with your tea. Argue about them, think about them, write some of your own. Find the millions of others buried in files, sitting on the tongue during love-making, flagging you down at family reunions. The Black women here are survivors, rulers, thinkers, warriors and changers, instigators, lovers, beauties and investigators, critics, planters, movers and shakers, navigators, lionesses and bears, feelers and princesses. Bondswomen speak among the architects, farmers among the artists, revolutionaries among the daughters. Among these words are hand grenades, African violets, fresh breezes, cassava flour and deep hugs—all necessary for survival. We are all here, calling out to and reaching one another, gathering at one another's feet and sharing the sustenance that has kept us alive and moving in the directions we must go. I wish to thank the following people for their assistance and encouragement during this project: my parents, Rene Dawson, Stephanie Byrd, Jera Ing-Odin, Rolanda Teal, Karen Willis, Donna Jones, Anne Courtney, and Tim Hall. I also wish to acknowledge the regretable omission of words from writers such as Octavia Butler, Gwendolyn Brooks, and Hattie Gossett, singers like Patti LaBelle and Anita Baker, photographer Elizabeth   Williams, and hundreds of other vital Black women of whom I am personally aware. Nevertheless, I give this collection—quotations and other words—to us, TO ALL OF US.

To the Elder Woman

When this black woman cook was asked for her recipes, she said, "I'll give you the recipes, but cooking is just like religion. Rules don't no more make a cook than sermons make a saint." I always remember that.

—Leah Chase

An old woman is never old when it comes to the dance she knows.

—Ibo proverb

Oh what makes my grandpa
love my grandma so
She's got the same old jelly
she had 40 years ago

—recorded by Cleo Gibson, blues singer, from "Nothing But the Blues," 1929

Don't let ol' folks tell you about the good ol' days. I was there. Where was they at?

—Jackie "Moms" Mabley

Today many older black women are respectfully addressed as "queen mothers."

—Jeanne Noble

¿Quién te dió morena vieja
esa hermosa gritería
que sale de tus pulmones
agitando noche y día
del mundo las sensaciones?

Old colored woman, who gave you
that strident melody
that comes from your lungs,
proclaiming night and day
the dramas of the world?

—Virginia Brindis de Salas from "Pregon   Numero Dos"
("Pregon #2")

As a girl we were required to enter my grandmother's house in the African way, so that if we had brought a little friend with us we had to first present them to my grandmother, who would inevitably ask, "Well, who are her people?" And then our friend would have to go down the line of her relations. If you walked into the house and you did not acknowledge the elders first, you were punished.

—bell hooks

W'en yu se ole wuman run, no ax wha'matter, run to.

When you see an old lady running, do not ask what is the matter, run too.

—Jamaican proverb

you's a black queen Sheba
great black great grandmom
i love the you
that works in my flesh

—Jodi Braxton from "Black Sheba"

We are old
when we rise against our times,
when we resist all change.
We are young as our dreams, our hopes
and our enthusiasm.
We are old as our fears,
our frustrations, our doubts.

—Septima P. Clark, activist

It is the duty of children to wait on elders, and not the elders on children.

—Kenyan proverb

Old people say, "Crown your efforts with success."
—Beulah Shepard Hester

USA TODAY: Many fans view you as a legend, almost a cult figure. Why?

LENA HORNE: A great deal of it has to do with curiosity. They want to see that an old woman can live, work and be entertaining. This is a very wonderful part of my life.

(Women's) faces are maps of the hardships they have gone through. The older women get, the prouder they should be.
—Sithembiso Nyoni

What an elder sees sitting, the young can't see standing.
—Ibo proverb

Most of these old ladies become reflective, so much so that they become living history books. They tell stories and sing songs of their historic past. They string together praise-names and retell the happenings of their community over and over again.
—Buchi Emecheta

What am I supposed to do with my 73 years of experience?
Am I supposed to bury it?

> —Juanita Jewel Craft

We will choose our most knowing
most eloquent old women
to spit in the mouths
of the newborn babies
so that they will remember....

> —Iyamide Hazeley from "When You Have
> Emptied Our Calabashes"

We often spend so much time bemoaning our loss of youth
that we fail to appreciate the charm, the serenity, and the grace
that can be ours as old women.

> —Dorothy R. Robinson, age 81, professional educator
> from Lavaca County, Texas

...these women with their hallelujah hearts
and pale saviors—these women
shall be our salvation.

> —Irma McClaurin from "Old Age Sequence"

When you kill the ancestor you kill yourself.

> —Toni Morrison

5

To Our Beauty

The blacker the berry the sweeter the juice.

—U.S. proverb

so pretty inside
there was a joy about her i had to be a woman
to understand

—Wanda Coleman from "Miss Jones"

To be a Black woman or a Black man and to retain one's
natural complexion is an act of demystification and
demythification. The colour black is not ugly.

—Awa Thiam

i have wrapped myself in my people's essence,
learned to wear Africa's stole
of dark, soft energy like night vapors
        rising from rainsoaked furrows;....

—Aneb Kgositsile from "Fourth Decade"

we "ourselves" are high art.

—Ntozake Shange

Randram-bao mahataitra.
Newly plaited hair attracts the eyes.

—Malagasy proverb

For news of the heart, ask the face.

—Hausa proverb

keep that isolate
natural   wild beauty
off the main roads   in the
mountains and like them,
don't   never   change.
                —doris davenport from "Cornelia to   Clarkesville"

Blacks are known to have very expressive eyes...A great deal of
nonverbal communication goes on among members of a
family...We're also said to have very smooth skin that is highly
sensitized....

—Dr. Alyce C. Gullattee, psychiatrist

Lidakho silira.

Buttocks cannot kill.
(Big Buttocks are not a disease.)

—Luyia saying

I have seen in the mirror
and the eyes of my sisters
that pretty is the woman in darkness
who follows with loving.
                    —Chirlane McCray from "I Used to Think"

INTERVIEWER: Do you have any preference
among the terms colored, Negro, black?

ALFREDA M. BARNETT: No. A rose by another name
smells just as sweet.

Ojo pa mi, ojo ko pa ewa ara mi danu.

The rain beats on me, but the rain cannot wash off the beauty
of my body.

—Yoruba proverb

¿De dónde provienes tú
apasionada, exaltada?
Tu sangre vio los ardores
de la Nigeria espectante.
Combada
y de ebano arrogante
el mapa de tu mirada.
Tus axilas aromadas
vegetación de la selva.
Paso de la culebra
tus caderas,
muchacha negra.

Where do you come from
passionate and exalted one?
Your blood saw the ardors
of expectant Nigeria.
Curved
and arrogant like the ebony
contour of your face.
Your fragrant armpits
like the flora of the jungle.
Like the undulation of the snake
your hips,
black girl.

      —Virginia Brindis de Salas from "Semblanza / Portrait"

Who say we no get beauty for Africa
Abi de pers'n dey craze
Abi e dey blind sef
            —Taiwo Olaleye-Oruene from "African Beauty"

Have you ever seen peaches
grow on a sweet potato vine
Just step in my back yard
and take a peep at mine
            —recorded by Trixie Smith, blueswoman,
                  from "Sorrowful Blues," 1924

Women are blessed with a jewel of strength that glows all
the time.
            —Judith Jamison

Obea ko aguare na wamma ntem a, na osiesie neho.

When a woman goes to bathe and is a long time in returning,
then (you can be sure) she is decking herself out.
            —Ashanti proverb

...and you loved
my skin
like black sand beaches;
my hair
like coconut fibres
my lips
large and generous
tasting of sun and fruit....
   —Jennifer Brown from "Africa and the Caribbean"

touch a black woman
you mistake for a rock and feel her
melting down to fudge

cradle a soft black woman
and burn fingers as you trace
revolution
beneath her woolly hair
    —Grace Nichols from "Of Course When They
   Ask For Poems About the 'Realities' Of Black Women"

Black folks developed the art of making-up. Our ancestors were extracting natural elements from the earth to adorn their bodies centuries ago...it's African...Hairstyling and making-up did not originate in the Western world; it was Black style first.
—Susan Taylor

put me
in a caftan
wrap my head
in silver
rub my face
with ochre
shod my feet
in gnu-hide
or nothing
give me a spear
in one hand
and a drum
in the other
sling a baby
on my back
place me
within the circle
of the sun

—Isetta Crawford Rawls from "Adah"

To Change

People who behave as though there's something wrong with
wanting to improve things are to me pathological....

—Florynce Kennedy

Ukwenza kuya emuva kuye phambili.

The doing moves backward then forward.

—Ndebele proverb

Your time is now, my sisters...New goals and new priorities,
not only for this country, but for all of mankind must be set.
Formal education will not help us do that. We must therefore
depend upon informal learning. We can do that by confronting people with their humanity aand their own inhumanity—
confronting them wherever we meet them: in the church, in
the classroom, on the floor of the Congress and the state
legislatures, in the bars, and on the streets. We must reject not
only the stereotypes that others hold of us, but also the stereotypes that we hold of ourselves.

—Shirley Chisholm

The forward movement of women of color almost always
initiates progressive change for all women.

—Angela Y. Davis

13

You never git nothing by bein' an angel child.
You better change yo ways and git real wild.
I'm gonna tell you something, wouldn't tell you no lie.
Wild women are the only kind that ever git by.
Wild women don't worry, they don't have no blues.
                              —Ida Cox, blueswoman, from
                              "Wild Women Don't Have the Blues"

I cannot change the world, but I do not have to conform.
                              —Marva Nettles Collins

We must begin to understand that a revolution entails not only the willingness to lay our lives on the firing line and get killed. In some ways, this is an easy commitment to make. To die for the revolution is a one-shot deal; to live for the revolution means taking on the more difficult commitment of changing our day-to-day patterns.

                              —Frances Beal

We are not responsible for changing the psyche of our oppressors; we are responsible, though, for fighting that oppression, for altering the oppression...for changing the circumstances of our lives and the constructs under which we live.

                              —Audre Lorde

So I am in church...and I went to the light and turned it off. I turned around and said, "Start praying for the light to come back on because there is current." So, they started to pray, saying "Please light, come" and nothing happened...Then I went and turned it on and I said: "There, it is not for God to do. It is for you to do. It is you who must do something about a situation to change it."

—Reverend Judith G. Weeks, born 10/28/24,
ordained minister of the Christ Circle for Better Living,
Trinidad and Tobago

It's essential that we understand that taking care of the planet will be done *as* we take care of ourselves. You know that you can't really make much of a difference in things until you change yourself.

—Alice Walker

Mundu muka na iguru itimenyagirwo.

Woman and sky cannot be understood.
(Woman, wind and fortune are ever changing.)

—Kikuyu proverb

Why there's a change in the weather
there's a change in the sea
But from now on
there'll be a change in me
I'm going to change my way of living
and that ain't no bluff
Why I'm thinking about changing
the way I got to strut my stuff

—recorded by Ethel Waters from
"There'll   Be Some Changes Made", 1921

It occurs to me that much organizational grief could be
avoided if people understood that partnership in misery does
not necessarily provide for partnership for change.

—June Jordan

Adult awareness gives us the power to change our mental tapes
and to re-parent ourselves in a different manner...Our lives
begin with loss, the loss of the security of our mother's womb.
To be able to truly cut the cords that bound me to both
parents has been the first step toward living my life in its
fullness.

—Linda H. Hollies

Garurira mbeu ti ya kinya kimwe.

Change! Seeds are not kept in one gourd.

—Gikuyu proverb

　　Sisters
git yr / blk / asses
out of that re
　　　　　volution
　　　　　　　ary's
bed.
　　that ain't no revolutionary
thing com / munal
　　　　　fuck/ing
ain't nothing political
bout fucking.

—Sonia Sanchez from "Memorial"

Redefining Blackness necessitates removing the artificial
boundaries that now exist among all Africans by thrashing out
the contradictions that created them. We would, then, rip
down the artificial boundaries of class, complexion, age—the
latest hang-up—and territorial limits to see that we do have
resources and that these resources do not in any way need to
be legitimized by the non-African world. We need only one
stamp—our own.

—Ann Cook

To Our Community

...the women in my community gave the lie to the mammy and the maid image....

—Erlene Stetson

Blackness is not a hair style. It is not a dashiki. Judge my blackness by the jobs that we have, by the money we are able to generate in the community in advance of the support services. Judge my blackness by that.

—Bertha Knox Gilkey

I don't care what diplomacy dictates. We have to stand up for our communities, to fight for them in new and different ways.

—Maxine Waters, assemblywoman

I think that if Black people don't work to get into a position where we can do something about our image and preserve what's true, it won't be done.

—Vinnette Carroll, Broadway actress, theatre producer and director

18

The timbre
in our voices
betray us
however far
we've been....

—Grace Nichols from "We New World Blacks"

What I really believe is that we as a people must be consciously
aware that we must perpetuate ourselves and some idea of
ourselves.

—Sherley Anne Williams

...we learned that service is the rent we pay for living. It is
the very purpose of life and not something you do in your
spare time.

—Marian Wright Edelman

...we are never permitted to forget the inequities of this
society. We can never rise to a level at which you are not
aware of what's going on in the black community. I think this
is something that is very characteristic of the life of the black
person in this country.

—Lucy Miller Mitchell

Black extended families and Black churches are two key institutions where Black women experts with concrete knowledge of what it takes to be self- defined Black women share their knowledge with the younger, less experienced sisters.

—Patricia Hill Collins

where I'm from
people take as much pride
in being from
where you're from
as anybody else.

—Stephanie Byrd from "Where You From"

I didn't want to write a poem that said "blackness
is," because we know better than anyone
that we are not one or ten or ten thousand things
Not one poem
We could count ourselves forever
and never agree on the number.

—Elizabeth Alexander from "Today's News"

Hard times are getting so much harder that it's forcing Black people to turn to one another. We had become so content and so "mind your business" till we found out that "mind your business" hasn't helped our survival as a community.

—Sister Souljah, rap vocalist

We grew up in a generation where people were concerned about what you were going to be, not just your name, because the race needed you. We were reared to believe a single failure was one that we could not afford...I hope we can regain that urgency.

—Bishop Leontine Kelly

We, Africans in America, come from people tied to the Earth, people of the drums which echo the
Earth's heartbeat...
People tied to soil and wind and rain as to each other....

—Aneb Kgositsile from "Part of Each
Other, Part Of the Earth"

...most of us have to wear some sort of mask outside our own group, and it's a relief to be able to put that mask down from time to time when we're back with our own kind.

—Althea Gibson Darben, b. 1927, Champion tennis player

Community empowerment means the strengthening of those who head households. In the inner city, that means organizing and empowering Black women.
> —Patrice Johnson, editor of *The Black Commentator*

...taking their cue from the feminist infra-structure of the black women's racial uplift movement, churchwomen created an institutional basis for women's self-consciousness. The result was an alternative model of power and leadership within the most authoritarian and least democratic of formal organizations—the episcopally governed church. These religious organizations transformed the negative and contradictory experiences of black women into an aspect of community life that maintained tradition and fostered social and individual change.
> —Cheryl Townsend Gilkes

We are positively a unique people. Breathtaking people. Anything we do, we do big! Despite attempts to stereotype us, we are crazy, individual and uncorral-able people.
> —Leontyne Price, b. 1927 in Laurel, Mississippi, "Prima Donna Absoluta"

The hand of a child can not reach the ledge; the hand of the elder can not enter the gourd: both the young and the old have what each can do for the other.
> —Yoruba proverb

To Our Courage

Women have belly and they would stand up, and all you man only study to go inside the rum shop. All you who want to go, go, cause all you dis is worms feedin on de union. We suffer so long here and we must sacrifice, and if we have to eat dirt we must eat it, and if we have to eat brick we must eat it, before we go back to that condition we was in, and if we have to eat grass we will eat grass.

> —Saheedan Ramroop, cane-cutter, born 2/14/1922, Trinidad and Tobago. Activist speaking to strikers who were buckling under pressure, 1975. As she said this, she bent down and furiously pulled a clump of grass and ate it. Mother of 10 children.

Zidele amathambo.

Give yourself up, bones as well.
(Take a chance!)

> —Ndebele proverb

Who wants to live with one foot in hell just for the sake of nostalgia? Our time is forever now!

> —Alice Childress

23

There is a way to look at the past. Don't hide from it. It will not catch you if you don't repeat it.

—Pearl Bailey

The young kids ask me why don't I wear an Afro. Well, I don't have to prove nothing. I got scars all over my body from all the struggles I been in.

—Florence Rice, tenant and consumer
organization activist, in Harlem, 1970

How to hang tough: Imagine yourself very cool,
very sharp, and altogether together. Remember, it's fine to be
crazy, it's like really okay to be crazy, like what the fuck
else we gon' do, we got so much heart, so much insight, we
livin' in a hellacious world, man, folks like us, if we wasn't
crazy, we'd be dead or crazy, ONE!

—Michelle T. Clinton from
"Manifestating the Rush / How To Hang"

There's nothing neat and tidy about me, like a nice social revolution. With me goes a mad, passionate, insane, scream-ing world of ten thousand devils and the man or God who lifts the lid off this suppressed world does so at his peril.

—Bessie Head

If you don't like my ocean
don't fish in my sea
Stay out of my valley
and let my mountain be
    —Ma Rainey, blueswoman, from "Don't Fish In My Sea"

The women of this world...must exercise leadership quality, dedication, concern, and commitment which is not going to be shattered by inanities and ignorance and idiots who would view our cause as one that is violative of the American dream of equal rights for everyone.
            —Barbara Jordan, born 1936, address, International
                Women's Year Conference,   Austin, TX, 1975

I think we should all be kicking ass fairly regularly, and one of my favorite targets is the media. I don't think we should continue to permit the Establishment to feed us only what they think we should have.

                            —Florynce Kennedy

...I am not a quitter. I will fight until I drop. That is a strength that is in my sinew...It is just a matter of having some faith in the fact that as long as you are able to draw breath in this universe you have a chance.

                            —Cicely Tyson

Be not discouraged black women of the world, but push
forward, regardless of the lack of appreciation shown you.
—Amy-Jacques Garvey, 1925

Women of Egypt and Libya
Drink her tears from River Nile
You will gain courage and bravery
Women of Congo and Liberia
Drink her tears from River Congo
You will shed inferiority
Women of Zambia and Zimbabwe
Drink her tears from River Zambezi
You will gain understanding
Women of South and West Africa
Drink her tears from River Limpopo
You shall see liberation

—Gcina Mhlope, South African poet,
from "We Are At War"

From my own study of the question, the colored woman
deserves greater credit for what she has done and is doing than
blame for what she cannot so soon overcome.
—Fannie Barrier Williams

I am deliberate
and afraid
of nothing.

> —Audre Lorde from "New Year's Day"

Are there no Shiphrahs, no Puahs among you, who will dare...to refuse to obey the *wicked laws* which require *woman to enslave, to degrade and to brutalize woman?* Are there no Miriams,...no Huldahs...Is there no Esther among you...?
> —Angelina E. Grimke from "An Appeal to the Christian Women of the South," American Anti-Slavery Society, 1836

We haven't got guns we haven't got nothing we are just going to fight with our talk—that's the only thing. We are not prepared to fly away like chickens.
> —Regina Ntongana, South African activist

...victory is often a thing deferred, and rarely at the summit of courage...What is at the summit of courage, I think, is freedom. The freedom that comes with the knowledge that no earthly power can break you; that an unbroken spirit is the only thing you cannot live without; that in the end it is the courage of conviction that moves things, that makes all change possible.
> —Paula Giddings

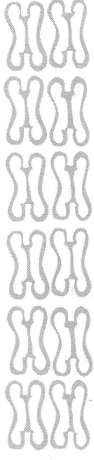

We are afraid to venture and I like bravery...If you can't do it, find out why you can't do it. Don't just stop and say, "Well, they are going to do what they want to do anyway, stay home"...It has done a lot of harm to us....
> —Christia Daniels Adair, suffragette and civil rights leader, politician for over 40 years in Texas. Born 10/22/1893.

The black sportswoman has attained her victories by overcoming barriers of a racial and sexual character which makes mere sporting opponents truly a piece of cake.
> —Dr. Carole A. Oglesby

Having overcome as a race and a sex so many obstacles that to the fainting, faltering heart seemed insurmountable in the past, we shall neither be discouraged at the temporary failures of our friends, not frightened at the apparent success of our foes.
> —Mary Church Terrell

It is better to protest than to accept injustice.
> —Rosa Parks

INTERVIEWER: What did they do when they saw you knock your mistress down?

SILVIA DUBOIS: Do! Why they were going to take her part, of course; but I just sat down the slop bucket and straightened up, and smacked my fists at 'em, and told 'em to wade in, if they dared, and I'd thrash every devil of 'em; and there wasn't a damned one that dared to come.

—born in New Jersey in 1768, bondswoman

Yize uvalo, inqobo yisibindi.

Fear is nothing, the real thing is courage.

—Ndebele proverb

...there was one of two things I had a right to, liberty or death. If I could not have one, I would have the other, for no man should take me alive.

—Harriet Ross Tubman (1820 - 1913)

The doll-baby type of woman is a thing of the past, and the wide-awake woman is forging ahead prepared for all emergencies, and ready to answer any call, even if it be to face the cannons on the battlefield.

—Amy-Jacques Garvey

29

Oh, teach me that life is to do and dare;
That the glory of life is not to spare
A boon that Now to the Future can lend,
Not even a soul, which, the right to defend,
Must venture to fathom the awful gloom,
Which lieth beyond the gate of the tomb.
Then shall I reckon that nothing is lost,
If freedom be gained, though blood is the cost....
                    —Sarah J. Foster from "Oh, Weave Me a Story"

Up to 1969, before I was—before then I had just been in and
out of prisons but then I was in solitary confinement for 17
months...it is then that I really felt made. It is such a hard test
of your ideals, and at the same time it teaches you so much of
what you stand for—your own values. Perhaps up to that stage
I had not realised the gravity of our struggle and up to that
stage, as a mother and as a black woman I wouldn't have
known what my reaction would be if I found myself in a
violent situation...But from that experience I know what I can
do in defence of this my country, in defence of what I believe
to be a just society. I believe that now.
                                        —Winnie Mandela

The woman who takes a woman lover lives dangerously in patriarchy.

—Cheryl Clarke

I know a woman who was arrested in 1976 who was very brash and aggressive. Nine policemen interrogated her the first night, and they said, "If you don't talk, we're going to rape you, one after the other." She replied, "Oh, great! The laws in this country never allowed me to have sex with a white guy. Who's going to be first?" And she started taking her clothes off, which totally shocked these guys, and they didn't do it.

—Elaine Mohamed, South African detainee in 1982

To Our Creativity

Art is a mystery. I didn't have no idea it was like it is. It is so particular. It's a great mystery. When I start a picture, I don't know no more what I'm going to do than you do.

—Minnie Jones Evans, artist, age 87

People *do* things, one of which might be writing, to help themselves and other people ask questions about who they are, who they might be, what kind of world they want to create, to remind ourselves that we do create the world.

—Barbara Christian

If you dance, you dance because you have to. Every dancer hurts, you know.

—Katherine Dunham

I suppose I think that the highest gift that man has is art and I am audacious enough to think of myself as an artist—that there is both joy and beauty and illumination and communion between people to be achieved through the dissection of personality.

—Lorraine Hansberry

Betty Carter eats up microphones by the dozens
Chews 'em up until they're part of her....
                    —Avotcja from "Who Is That Lady???"

Black women, whose experience is unique, are seldom recognized as a particular social-cultural entity and are seldom
thought to be important enough for serious scholarly consider-
ation. This invisibility, however, means that the opportunities
for creative research are infinite.

                    —Barabara Smith

Music comes first from my heart, and then goes upstairs to my
head where I check it out.

                    —Roberta Flack, pianist, composer, vocalist

It is a risk to connect. But the artist—the one the Creator
shows—does so. With the understanding that connection
itself is simply the expression of her or his being, and that not
to at least make the effort is to die.

                    —Alice Walker

INTERVIEWER: You sound like a very independent lady. How do you feel about the critics who look at your paintings? If they say they are not good, do you care?

CLEMENTINE HUNTER: I don't care how it is. If they want 'em, just let 'em get 'em, and if they don't, they can leave 'em there.

To express and create, one must have lived, I mean in the sense of tasting the fruit of the forbidden tree.
—Afrakuma Bannerman, oil painter, Ghana

If there is a single distinguishing feature of the literature of black women-and this accounts for their lack of recognition—it is this: their literature is about black women; it takes the trouble to record the thoughts, words, feelings, and deeds of black women, experiences that make the realities of being black in America look very different from what men have written.
—Mary Helen Washington, one of the pioneers in Black women's literary tradition

The truth is that the need for realism in art is actually a part of me and I don't need to excuse it with the idea that my audience isn't "ready" for anything more "modern." They are accepting works of pure form. After all, abstract art was born in Africa....
—Elizabeth Catlett

Black music is the outcome of our attitude and it is constantly evolving through our social life and environment. Black music is an American prodigy....
—Clora Bryant, vocalist and trumpeter

The responsibility of the chronicler is to hear what people truly are saying about their experiences. To use their rhythm and cadence of expression to define and describe and not delete it from the retelling.
—Barbara Omolade

It is a real fact that wherever you want anything done, teach a woman how to do it and in a few days you will have the same thing in various beautiful uncountable numbers.
—Councillor Rushwaya for Shurugwi, Zimbabwe, 1983

My very first lessons in the art of telling stories took place in, of all places, the kitchen of a brownstone in Brooklyn...Every afternoon my mother and three or four of her friends would gather in the kitchen around an oilcloth-covered table and talk...They didn't just gossip...And they told stories...with effortless art and technique. They were natural-born storytellers in the oral tradition.

—Paule Marshall

Let us not deceive ourselves. Africans have learned an imperialist view of history which negated the African past and treated our literary tradition as inferior "folk" literature. We have been victimized especially by Western imperialist criticism, which intimates that our African writers cannot stand up aesthetically to these European writers. This is a serious fallacy.
—Dr. Micere Mugo, Kenyan intellectual
and academic critic, 1976

It might be said that the genuine poetry of the black women appeared not in literature (during the Harlem Renaissance) but in the lyrics of blues singers like Bessie Smith. Female blues singers...wrote about the black woman's autonomy and vulnerability, sexuality and spirituality.

—Barbara Christian

spread your legs, your arms, let your
hair go bad and
dance, poet, sing,
sculpt, paint, fight.

it's alright woman.
it's alright woman.
it's alright woman
it's alright woman.
　　　　　—Safiya Henderson from "Portrait of a Woman Artist"

Now, I carry these poems
in my pockets, like necessary
change, keep the words in
my mouth, alive.
　　　　　—Valerie Jean from "Psalm of Empowerment"

I had developed a new light in my painting, which I called
Black Light, a way of looking at us that came out of our new
"black is beautiful" sense of ourselves. My palette was all dark
colors...But next to each other the dark tones of reds, greens,
blues, brown, and grays came alive, no matter how subtle the
nuance.

　　　　　—Faith Ringgold

To Our Culture

Culture is not limited to the West, or Europe or a white skin or Christianity. Culture, in its truest sense, in its universal sense is the expression of the *personality* of a people.

—Bessie Head

Everybody knows about "the kitchen" because when we were little girls sitting between those knees that served like locks, when they came with that brush or comb, you got ready because they would inevitably get to "the kitchen," the nape of the neck,...

—Johnnetta Betsch Cole

I'll bet you could measure individual blacks' degrees of radicalism in their lives with a dated record of their age and changing hairstyles.

—Carol Talbot

Move your neck according to the music.

—Ethiopian-Galla proverb

...black women must speak in a plurality of voices as well as in a multiplicity of discourses.

—Mae Gwendolyn Henderson

we propose to speak
your language
but not abandon ours;
we insist that you understand
that you do not
understand us.
You may begin
by not shouting—
we are tired of noise.

—Pamela Mordecai from "Protest Poem"

After the birth of each of my granmother's five children the
cord was buried and orange trees planted near the house.
These trees now bear the names of her children.

—Michelle Cliff, poet and writer, scholar

Right off the boat, we took the lean, tight-butted, matter-of-
fact foreign parlance we heard and made it into a voluptuous,
vital, moving tongue of our own. We filled it with rhythm; we
be word dancers. We used it to deceive, confuse and conceal
information. Talking, for us, became a verbal game with
African rules.

—Vertamae Smart-Grosvenor, writer

Beauty shops
could have been
a hell-of-a-place
            to ferment
    a   revolution.
                —Willi M. Coleman from "Among the
                        Things That Use To Be"

Soul food you see, can't always be measured by the cup,
It's a little of this and a little of that and see what comes up.
                —Reverend Mother Charleszetta Waddles

Signifying is a skill, a method of disengagement which allows
you to unwind.

                                        —bell hooks

Emotion indicates that a speaker believes in the validity of an
argument... expressiveness should be reclaimed and valued.
                                —Patricia Hill Collins

No one should take off my gown in the market place, then,
come to my house and offer to put it back on me.
                                        —Ibo proverb

40

We are always asked to celebrate the new and improved laundry detergent as though that which came out yesterday is already obsolete. And we carry this habit, this outlook, into our daily lives. This is extremely dangerous.

—Toni Cade Bambara

When I think of hip-hop, I think of Africa, and I think of the drummers setting the tone for life. When there was an enemy in the village, you had to have a fast drum beat, telling you to prepare for war, telling you that the enemy's coming. I think of hip-hop as a war drum.

—Sister Souljah, rap vocalist

In several African communities, women dominate as musicmakers...Foreordained women become poet-musicians and are usually respected composers of songs paid handsomely by the chiefs....

—Mildred Denby Green

If you say Motown didn't teach you to slow dance, you're lying, pure and simple.

—Patricia Smith from "Sweet Daddy"

USA TODAY: Often you sing and then you stop and preach. Why?

SHIRLEY CAESAR: I do it because I'm a preacher. And I like to paint pictures. If I can't pull that picture out of a song then I paint that picture with words. I want them to see what my song is saying.

       the fact that we are an
interdisciplinary culture / that we understand more than verbal communication / lays a weight on afro-american writers that few others are lucky enough to have been born into. we can use with some skill virtually all our physical senses / as writers commited to bringing the world as we remember it / imagine it / & know it to be...

—Ntozake Shange

We have the ability as a race to speak in tongues, to dream in tongues, to love in tongues. We have that. We do it. That's what excites me in terms of how we communicate.

—Alexis DeVeaux, writer

you can shake
just like it would a tree
The way you shake it
it's pleasing me
Just let me tell you
a thing or two
A plenty of people shake it
but not like you

—recorded by Anna Bell, blues singer,
from "Shake It, Black Bottom," 1928

For ordinary African-American women, those individuals who
have lived through the experiences about which they claim to
be experts are more believable and credible than those who
have merely read or thought about such experiences.

—Patricia Hill Collins

Whoever wants to be admired at a festival, should be prepared
to dance well.

—Ibo proverb

The subtle ways in which black people communicate with each other, unperceived by the outsider—or, if perceived, likely to be misinterpreted—are nevertheless the cues that make for effective communication.

—Annette Powell Williams, then a graduate student at Northeastern Illinois University's Center for Inner City Studies

Oh the blues ain't nothing
but a good woman feeling bad
                    —recorded by Georgia White, blueswoman, 1938

If a vegetable is meant to be eaten raw, then it should be raw, but if not, it should be honestly cooked.

—Edna Lewis, cook

I need kai kai   ah
a glass of akpetesie   ah
from torn arm of Bessie Smith   ah
                    —Jayne Cortez from "Kai Kai (For the Poets)"

…I particularly appeal to readers who are female and black, to continue the examination of your life experiences, to identify the threads of style, authenticity, strength and sensitivity running through them, to value them and share them (whether wanted or not by those around you) in whatever form is yours, in stories, in performing, in formal speeches, or in research.

—Dr. Carole A. Oglesby

If I actually ran the world, I'd do it from the kitchen. It's not anything deliberate or a statement or anything, that's just how I understand things. It's arranged along informal lines.

—Jamaica Kincaid

The whole of a woman's life in Africa is controlled by ritual, from the day you are born to the day you die.

—Rosemary Edet, member of the Circle of Concerned African Women Theologians, Nigeria, 1992

…our turn to Africa should, hopefully, be for the richness of its culture,…for regeneration.

—Ann Cook

To the Daughters

You pause, just ready to grow up.
Your smile says—I will be a woman
like you, my smile says, you are
pure delight. In that flash
of love and homage we know
it is sweet to be female.

—Christine Craig from "Island"

Down through the ages, the image of majesty has come to the black girl in the admonition: "Walk proud! You are the descendant of queens!"

—Jeanne Noble

I do feel strongly that there is a necessity to be selfish at the point of trying to save a little bit of yourself for yourself. That is the only way, and I keep telling my daughter this, that the only way she can really be useful to herself, to her child and to her husband, and to others is even if nobody else agrees, and if it looks as if you're being hard-hearted, take a little time to restore your own soul.

—Muriel S. Snowden

Daughters were to give
Mothers
A sense of themselves.

> —Sindamani Bridglal from "She Lives
> Between Back Home and Home"

Going to get some eating dirt, special dirt
For my mother.
Going to take a pill, a fork
And dig in the special ground,
Until the pail is full
With baked brown, sweet soil.

> —Karen Mitchell from "The Eating Hill"

I remember somebody asking my grandmother "why do you
educate your daughters? They will all get married in the end"
and she said "Because when they have children they will also
educate them."

> —Ruth Nita Barrow, nursing educator,
> born 11/15/1916 in Barbados

You are the child of wind and ravens I created
always my daughter

> —Audre Lorde from "Progress Report"

47

I am Diamonane, beloved
daughter, bird child of obsidian and serpent. I am the
egg, the sperm.
> —Colleen J. McElroy from "A Woman's Song"

The relationship between an African- American mother and
her adolescent daughter carries with it a challenge: from the
mother's point of view, she feels a responsibility to encourage
great maturity at a relatively fast rate; thus the saying, "raising
daughters but loving sons" is at the core of her attention.
> —Mary C. Lewis

Owarungirwe na nyina tarungirwa.

She who learned from her mother how to fry doesn't like
others frying for her.
> —Kigezi proverb, southwest Uganda

…to stand and say
before you all
the child was black and female and
therefore mine
> —Claire Harris from "Policeman Cleared in
> Jay-Walking Case"

To Our Dreams

My ancestors dream to me
  'Come'
and showed me the magic blackness…
     —Maureen Ismay from "My Grandmother"

We must hear the voices and have the dreams of those who came before us, and we must keep them with us in a very real sense. This will keep us centered. This will help us to maintain our understanding of the job we must do. And if we do the job we must do, then we will win.

     —Sonia Sanchez

Nothing is achieved in a dream.

     —Malinke proverb

We need to dig and jump into the land we come from; one woman after another, one dream upon the other, calling up who we are.

     —Ntozake Shange

49

I feel that one needs to have dreams come true. If you aim at the sky and you get to the tree top then you are never too low.
—Millicent Iton, Director of CANSAVE, a human service organization. Born 4/3/1928, St. Vincent and the Grenadines.

…I believe that you cannot go any further than you can think. I certainly believe if you don't desire a thing, you will never get it.
—Charleszetta Waddles

I do not regret the time and energy consumed in serving others. I can not help wondering, however, whether I might not have succeeded as a short-story writer, or a novelist, or an essayist, if the conditions under which I lived had been more conducive to the kind of literary work I so longed to do.
—Mary Church Terrell

Our dreams are the most accessible way to communicate with the ancestors.
—Luisah Teish

The least I can say for myself is that I forcefully created for myself, under extremely hostile conditions, my ideal life. I took an obscure and almost unknown village in the Southern African bush and made it my own hallowed ground. Here, in the steadiness and peace of my own world, I could dream dreams a little ahead of the somewhat vicious clamour of revolution and the horrible stench of evil social systems.

—Bessie Head

A novel is something you have to reflect on; you have to create it, you have to have characters, interplay of characters, it has to reflect what goes on in your society,…And you have to dream about it and black women do not have time to dream.

—Miriam Tlali

Who said that I
Was content to shop
For vinyl handbags
In a Graham Avenue
Discount Store?

—Yvonne C. Gregory from "Who Said?"

I always believed that if you set out to be successful, then you already were.

> —Katherine Dunham at age 81 in 1990. Created one of the first professional Black dance companies.

Never fail yourself
Never commit to limits…
        Follow
the particulars of your spirit
as they pull you….

> —veronica d. cunningham, poet

I was going to buy a farm, buy me a big farm…I was going to build them a house that didn't have tin on the top, a house that had rooms to it. I wasn't going to have the pigpen in the backyard, and I wasn't going to have the chickens roosting under the house…We were going to have good shortening corn bread…and we were going to have fried chicken. And I was going to be sure I threw away the neck and the head…I was going to have brown gravy, and I was *not* going to have that white gravy…And I was certainly going to make it myself so I wasn't going to let no flies get in.

> —Anita Stroud, b. 1900 in slavery in South Carolina. Age 80.

The highest mountain can't be raced,
it's something you must slowly climb.
                    —recorded by Ida Cox, blues singer, from
                                "One Hour Mama"

…Only through these dreams
are we ourselves: all that we
may hope to be, locked in
our day-long longing for night.
                    —Sarah Webster Fabio from
                        "All Day We've Longed for Night"

No person has the right to rain on your dreams.
                    —Marian Wright Edelman

Ahu okunda tihashweka muhanda.

The path to your heart's desire is never overgrown.
                    —Kigezi proverb, southwest Uganda

Kitchens, broom closets and dust rags are not in her dreams.
                    —Colleen J. McElroy from "Day Help"

...yuh can fine she
gazin cross de water
a stick
eena her han
trying to trace
a future
in de san

—Jean Binta Breeze from "Dreamer"

We have to do whatever we have to do in order for there to be
a new day. That means dealing with practical reality in a way
that keeps you very close to the ground, always knowing what
you have to deal with in the everyday sense...Maybe you
propel your dreams two or three generations down the line.
Lay it on your daughters or your sons or their children. You
understand that what you have to do is make up the difference,
whatever that is.

—Bernice J. Reagon

It was this peaceful world of black people simply dreaming in
their own skins that I began to slowly absorb into my own life.
It was like finding black power and black personality in a
simple and natural way.

—Bessie Head

To Family

Parents honor parents.

—Malagasy proverb

I was inspired by my father, who gave me faith in myself and the learned ability to keep my mouth shut, while accomplishing obstacles others were still talking about doing.

—Era Bell Thompson, known as the "Dean of Black Women Magazine Journalists"

Olwikho sineingubo!

Blood relationship is not like a dress (which you take off and put on at your leisure!)

—Luyia saying

...any strategies intended to alleviate the prevailing problems among poor Black people that methodologically target the family for change and leave the socioeconomic conditions perpetuating Black unemployment and poverty intact are doomed to failure from the outset.

—Angela Y. Davis

...individual homosexuals have been a part of the Black race during our entire history on this continent. We have worked together, worshipped together, and together faced loneliness—all within the context of Black family life—and we have survived as the Black Family to this very day.
—June Dobbs Butts, Ed.D., then asst. professor, Dept. of Psychiatry at Howard University College of Medicine, 1981.

Cia mucii iri gacuguma ga cio na muthuuri wa cio.

Family affairs have got their own code and their own elder.
—Gikuyu proverb

I was so tiny when I started playing...that I would stand between my Daddy's knees, and I would beg him to get my guitar. So he would lay it on the bed for me, and then I would stand up by the bed and play about three frets down on the guitar. Oh, I would look at Daddy, and he had such a smile! I can see it now, the smile he had on his face when I would make a good chord. He would holler, "That's my girl!"
—Etta Reid Baker, blues guitarist, age 66.

E je k'a s' oro ile wa o.

Let us practice the rituals of our family.
—Yoruba saying

Within my own family my great grandmother was a great composer of family poetry. And her poetry pieces came down the family line, so much so that my mother and my grandmother would often recite this poetry on various occasions in the family. For instance, if they had quarrelled, they would use this poetry in their peace offerings.

—Lauretta Ngcobo

my family's hot-buttered love has been
         aging for years, now;
let's open these mason jars
and set their spirits free.

—Leslie Reese from "freedom music"

This is one of our most serious problems when we consider the politics of eugenics. The questions…arise as to who makes the decision whether one is emotionally sound, and who sets the criteria for the number of children that constitutes the "ideal" family.

—Dr. Alyce C. Gullattee, psychiatrist

The family with not enough income cannot maintain good family conditions.

—Lucy Miller Mitchell

57

From the days of the slave traders down to the present, the Negro woman has had the responsibility of caring for the needs of the family, of militantly shielding it from the blows of Jim Crow insults, of rearing children in an atmosphere of lynch terror, segregation, and police brutality, and of fighting for an education for the children.

—Claudia Jones, member of the Communist Party

If relatives help each other, what evil can hurt them?

—Ethiopian proverb

Black people, both during and after the slave era, have been compelled to build, creatively and often improvisationally, a family life consistent with the dictates of survival.

—Angela Y. Davis

My father was our teacher, and he taught us the history of our country. "This is what you are going to find in the text," he would say. "This is how the white man wrote your history. But I am telling you that, contrary to what this white man says, it is so and so. These books were written to condition you into believing that the whites are your masters." I learned this for the first time from my own father.

—Winnie Mandela

To Our Feminism

A black feminist ideology…declares the visibility of black women…Second, black feminism asserts self-determination as essential. Black women are empowered with the right to interpret our reality and define our objectives. Third, a black feminist ideology fundamentally challenges the interstructure of the oppressions of racism, sexism, and classism both in the dominant society and within movements for liberation. Finally, a black feminist ideology presumes an image of black women as powerful, independent subjects.

—Deborah K. King

Hit one ring and the whole chain will resound.

—Sotho proverb

If the man may preach, because the Savior died for him, why not the woman? seeing he died for her also. Is he not a whole Savior, instead of a half one? as those who hold it wrong for a woman to preach, would seem to make it appear.

—Jarena Lee, b. free at Cape May, NJ, 1783. Preacher, traveled 2325 miles and delivered 178 sermons in a single year when over age 40

As a blackwoman
the personal is political
hold no empty rhetoric.

> —Maud Sulter from "As A Black Woman"

Feminism is aggressive, but it is the aggression of revolution.

> —Awa Thiam

Black feminism and Black Lesbianism are not interchangeable. Feminism is a political movement and many Lesbians are not feminists. Although it is also true that many Black feminists are not Lesbians, this myth has acted as an accusation and a deterrent to keep non- Lesbian Black feminists from manifesting themselves, for fear it will be hurled against them.

> —Barbara Smith

Feminism has become the shorthand for the proclamation that women's experience should become an integral part of what goes into the definition of being human.

> —Mercy Amba Oduyoye

Feminism that denies freedom of ethnic and cultural differences is not feminism….

> —Julia A. Boyd

Uhii ni uumagwo no uka ndumagwo.

Boyhood passes, but womanhood lasts forever.
—Gikuyu proverb

You know, it would probably be easier for me not to speak out, not to ever say anything about the issues of sexual harassment or the role of women in the workplace and politics, not talk about those things ever again in life. But I think it would be irresponsible for me not to say what I really believe in my heart to be true—that there are some serious inequities we face as women and that we can work to address these inequities. I will not be satisfied anymore with living my life simply for myself. Other issues are much broader than my own little world.
—Anita Hill

The emotional, sexual and psychological stereotyping of females begins when the doctor says: "It's a girl."
—Shirley Chisholm

The most popular justification black women had for not becoming feminists was their hatred of white women.
—Michele Wallace

The days are gone when men were seen to be the indispensable spice of life!

—Councillor Mukweha from Kadoma Town
Council, Zimbabwe, 1983

Silence is the door of consent.

—Berber proverb

Religion, science, art, economics, have all needed the feminine flavor; and literature, the expression of what is permanent and best in all of these, may be gauged by any time to measure the strength of the feminine ingredient.

—Anna Julia Cooper

Often we are told that we have an option, that if we don't want to be a mammy, we can be a "lady." But we have already learnt something from the white women who are now saying plenty about this "lady" business.

—Margaret Prescod-Roberts

There ain't but 3 men
who really can spend my dough
There's the rent man, the grocery man
and the man that owns the clothing store
                    —Alice Moore, blues singer, from "Three Men"

Every woman has got a talent and should practice it freely.
                    —Violet Chidarara

Feminism has very little to do with the kind of clothes you
wear, whether you wash dishes or not. It's got to do with how
you see yourself in relation to other people, whether you are
oppressive or exploitative….
                    —Rozena Maart

…giving people choices enhances our capacity to attain dignity
and reach our capacity as productive human beings.
                    —Faye Wattleton

Though not philosophers, we long since learned that equality
before the law, euality in the best sense of that term under our
institutions, is totally different from social equality.
                    —Fannie Barrier Williams

Strange that the word Amazon, when associated with black women (or any other woman, for that matter), carries negative connotation. It is associated with the attitude that it is unfeminine for women to fight, which is quite different from the attitude that neither men nor women should fight or wage wars.

—Jeanne Noble

I will not be called a feminist here, because it is European. It is as simple as that, I resent that...I don't like being defined by them...I do believe in the African kind of feminism. They call it womanism, because, you see, you Europeans don't worry about water, you don't worry about schooling, you are so well off. Now, I buy land, and I say, "O.K., I can't build on it, I have no money, so I give it to some women to start planting." That is my brand of feminism.

—Buchi Emecheta

If Elizabeth can run England, I can run America as president. What has she got that I didn't used to have, and can't get again?

—Jackie "Moms" Mabley, comedienne, c. 1894 - 1975

...we must try to teach the people that women's problems are the nation's concerns.

—Julia Zvobgo

The black woman had had to struggle against being a person of great strength.

—Dorothy Height

The European feminist struggle is not exactly the same as that of an African woman. Their struggles may be similar, but they begin from two differing positions…The African woman is supposed to offer a tremendous service to society, over and above the mothering of her children. She has to work hard for it, she has to provide food.

—Lauretta Ngcobo

Foolish men, who accuse woman without reason, without seeing that you are yourselves the cause of the very thing that you blame!

—Sor Juana Ines de la Cruz, 1651 - 1695, from "Roundels," c. 1670. Considered among the best early Mexican poets.

Feminism—the belief that women are full human beings capable of participation and leadership in the full range of human activities—intellectual, political, social, sexual, spiritual and economic. Feminism is to sexism what black nationalism is to racism; the most rational response to the problem.

—Pearl Cleage

...I asked a young White woman why she was studying social anthropology. She replied that she was hoping to go to Zimbabwe, and felt she could help women there by advising them how to organize. The Black women in the audience gasped in astonishment. Here was someone scarcely past girlhood, who had just started university and had never fought a war in her life. She was planning to go to Africa to teach female veterans of a liberation struggle how to organize! This is the kind of arrogant, if not absurd attitude we encounter repeatedly. It makes one think: Better the distant armchair anthropologists than these "sisters."

—Ifi Amadiume

Some feminists feel that a woman should never be wrong. We have a right to be wrong.

—Alice Childress

The world can not move without woman's sharing in the movement, and to help give a right impetus to that movement is woman's highest privilege.

—Frances E. W. Harper, born 1825.
Lecturer and advocate for the aspirations
of black women

To Our Health

It is more blessed to give than to receive, so give to *yourself* as much as you can as often as you can.
—LaVerne Porter Wheatley Perry, clinical psychologist

Ekitagambirwe kizimba aha mutima.

Repressed feelings swell the heart.
—Kigezi proverb, southwest Uganda

whatever loving took out of her
she stayed up nights
trying to give it back to herself….
—Leslie Reese from "after"

I believe racism has killed more people than speed, heroin, or cancer, and will continue to kill until it is no more.
—Alice Childress

Learn to be quiet enough to hear the sound of the genuine within yourself so that you can hear it in other people.
—Marian Wright Edelman

One of the things that black women have started talking about…is that many of us are like empty wells; we give a lot, but we don't get much back. We're asked to be strong…I am so tired of that stuff.

—Byllye Y. Avery

I was raised on pork, and believe me, I'm healthy.

—Tina Turner

Being a black woman means frequent spells of impotent, self-consuming rage.

—Michele Wallace

You are the only person who can forgive yourself. Once that forgiving has taken place, you can then console yourself with the knowledge that a diamond is the result of extreme pressure…The pressure can make you into something quite precious, quite wonderful, quite beautiful and extremely hard.

—Maya Angelou

After distress, solace.

—Swahili proverb

Under the auspices of denial, incest becomes the measure of an absolute negativity....

—Hortense J. Spillers

I like to laugh, I like to have a great time. But I also have a right to my anger, and, I don't want anybody telling me I shouldn't be, that it's not nice to be, and that something's wrong with me because I get angry.

—Maxine Waters

You make your disgrace, your shame, work for you.

—Ai from "Evidence: From A Reporter's Notebook"

Little with health is better than much with sickness.

—Berber proverb

I've found that grief is as private and personal as handwriting... And imitating somebody else's doesn't make it your own.

—Bridgett M. Davis

The thing to do is to grab the broom of anger and drive off the beast of fear.

—Zora Neale Hurston

Omugabuzi ayebanza.

The giver starts with herself.

> —Kigezi proverb, southwest Uganda

…I am perfectly willing to expose a great deal of my foolishness because I don't think that infallibility is anything to be proud of. I don't believe that I should be perfect.

> —Nikki Giovanni, poet

Attendants of the sick person know the name of the sickness.

> —Ibo proverb

I am not a Black Goddess
I cannot save you
I am not a Black Devil
I cannot destroy you
There is   Healing in my arms….

> —Kate Rushin from "The Black Goddess"

I have always marveled at the fact that some Black people consider abortion and birth control as genocidal, when to me, they are the precise things that might enable a Black woman to take control of her life.

> —Beverly Smith

Kushala bunke kwipapa.

Remaining alone is carrying oneself.
(No matter how strong someone may be, she can't do everything by herself.)

—Kaonde proverb

Compete, don't envy.

—Berber proverb

Kanyoni kabariti keminagira njoya.

The bird that flaps its wings too much will drop its feathers.
(Generosity without limit will exhaust one's resources.)

—Gikuyu proverb

This social process of destructive distortion is achieved through the imposition, from birth to death, of a stressful, negative and non-supportive social/environmental experience upon the people who are to be inferiorized.

—Dr. Frances Cress Welsing

Hate has no medicine.

—Ghanian (Accra) proverb

She who conceals her disease cannot expect to be cured.

—Ethiopian proverb

There has been silence about…the pressure from all sides to be perfect, to perform beyond all expectancies, or forget it. When one is held at all times to be representative of one's self, one's family, and one's race, the cost of failure may make a contest quite unworth the attempt.

—Dr. Carole A. Oglesby

If you try to cleanse others—like soap, you will waste away in the process!

—proverb from Madagascar

Hopelessness is a Black female learned attitude. Black females chronically appear depressed—what we call low-level depression in my field. That means you ain't depressed enough to really go crazy, you're working too hard to have time to think about killing yourself….

—LaVerne Porter Wheatley Perry, clinical psychologist

Try this bracelet: if it fits you wear it; but if it hurts you, throw it away no matter how shiny.

—Kenyan proverb

…there is an element of Play that is almost ritualistic in Black folk life. It serves to mediate the tensions, stress, and pain of constant exploitation and oppression.

—bell hooks

Coping is not to be interpreted as being hardened to the effects of adversity. We certainly are vulnerable to being moved by such things as sorrow, loneliness, neglect, unhappiness, and even by happiness. But we are also capable of finding the means or, rather, the alternatives for developing and maintaining our emotional stability by feeling good about ourselves, at least some of the time, while living in a society that is not in tune with being black and/or with being female—and at the same time!

—Lena Wright Myers

i need no takers
to leave me half empty
i'd rather be alone
half full

—Nikki Grimes from "The Takers"

I was seeking mental health, social adjustment, mature realism, self- actualization, empowerment and all the other psycho-babble concepts. Twelve years later, I can see all that meant I was looking for my bitch. And I found her. And I'm happy to have her on my side.

—Judy Simmons, editor and writer

you can put the blahs in a no name box
and mark it
don't open until never.

—Carolyn M. Rodgers from "Folk"

I don't drink or do any drugs. I never have and I never will. I don't need them. I'm a Black woman from the land of the free, home of the brave and I figure I don't need another illusion.

—Bertice Berry

Ezikubingire nizo zikworeka omuhanda.

The troubles that chase you away also show the road.

—Kigezi proverb, southwest Uganda

A way out of no way is too much to ask,
Too much of a task for any one woman.

—from song "Oughta Be A Woman", words by June Jordan

To Our Herstories

If our people are to fight their way up out of bondage we must arm them with the sword and the shield and the buckler of pride—belief in themselves and their possibilities, based upon a sure knowledge of the achievements of the past.
—Mary McLeod Bethune

It would seem that in order to qualify as heroine or leader, a Black woman's life must be one of personal loss, denial and sacrifice.
—Marcia Ann Gillespie, writer and editor

I don't walk "correct" because I want to be super righteous. I simply want to say to the world—through my actions—that Black women, having endured, are certainly women who should be revered…respected on the stage of history.
—Sonia Sanchez

I am Black, America has cause to be proud.
—Barbara Buckner Wright

...let's learn / how to fight
how to document / our existence
so no more / children
will come / behind
us / thinking
we didn't / exist,....

—Sapphire from "Yellow"

(1964)
I'm just wondering if this isn't the story of the Negro girls in
the Olympics: They pulled themselves up beyond where they
really were supposed to be.

—Earlene Brown, Olympian

...despite the importance of W. C. Handy, generally desig-
nated as "Father of the Blues," it was black women singers of
the 1920's who made blues history.

—D. Antoinette Handy

To console myself, I make a list of
every black woman writer who has
ever written a book that I have
read—or even heard of.
The list goes on for twenty-seven pages.
    —Becky Birtha from "Poem from a Clerk in the Law Library"

…in knowing and reconstructing our stories, however problematic, to tell them so that others may hear them, we have the burden not just of these stories, but of *herstory* itself.
>—Abena P. A. Busia

…I know that we must reclaim those bones in the Atlantic Ocean…All those people who said "no" and jumped ship…We don't have a marker, an expression, a song that we all use to acknowledge them…we have all that power that we don't tap; we don't tap into the ancestral presence in those waters.
>—Toni Cade Bambara

We need to uncover and (re)write our own multistoried history, and talk to one another as we are doing so.
>—Gloria T. Hull

The whole Civil War and the vintage years of slavery are our RECENT history. As activist women—black, white, brown, yellow—we have to re-examine our history to determine what's really past and what isn't.
>—Jennifer Henderson, activist, age 37 in 1986

We are still fighting the same battles, because we have not studied our history enough to avoid making the same mistakes.
>—Pat Parker, poet and activist

Who were my great-grandparents? Where did *they* come from? Were they slaves? And *their* parents, where did *they* come from? My daughter was demanding her past, but I could not give it to her without discovering my own.

—D. S. Redford

Indeed, Africa produced some of the first fighting women generals.

—Dr. Frances Cress Welsing

I ask:
where is our voice?
where are the ghosts wearing our lips and our sound?
so that we can do something about this amnesia….

—Leslie Reese from "ghosts"

…in 1962, from the diggings of Olduvai Gorge, Tanzania, the Leakeys unearthed the fossil that helped forge the links of probability into near certainty that humans, as we know them today, did begin life in Africa. What further made the Leakey's discovery of interest was that it established this fossil as a concrete record of a female who had lived approximately 800,000 years ago…"Homo habilis woman," meaning "woman with ability," …all abilities which mark the history of the black woman.

—Jeanne Noble

True emancipation lies in the acceptance of the whole past, in deriving strength from all my roots.

—Pauli Murray

Rites and rituals, along with intuition, feelings, seeing, speaking, and singing embody a tremendous repertoire of historical methods. The griot-historian who recognizes and uses these methods as well as reading and writing is in opposition to the paradigm of Western intellectual history and its civilization.

—Barbara Omolade

The Ashanti of Ghana and other people in West Africa have an icon. It is the image of a bird that looks backward and the feet of the bird are pointing forward. This symbolizes that a people must be rooted in their past if they are to move forward. How can you possibly know how far you can go if you have no sense of how far you have been?…If they don't know, they will assume the myths they have learned in America are true.

—Niara Sudarkasa

Day is short as ever; time's as long as it has been.

—Geechee proverb

History don't stop to let nobody out of it. So go ahead, and get into the facts. Then we can move on.

—June Jordan

Many of the stories that we don't hear much of are about the mammies who would slip poison in the food of the masters, the mammy providing hiding places for runaways....

—Margaret Prescod-Roberts

Too much of our history is consigned to anonymity, which makes it all the more desirable that we humanize our past, whenever possible, by bringing alive the names and faces of those who went before us.

—Sisters in Study from *Charting the Journey*

She tells me:
don't write things down
cause then it belongs to the paper.
Keep it safe inside.
Best to pass information
like blood through veins.

—Thylias Moss from "Some History, Some
Prophecy, Some Truth"

I, me, I am a free black woman.
My grandmothers and their mothers
knew this and kept their silence
to compost up their strength,
kept it hidden
and played the game of deference
and agreement and pliant will.

It must be known now how that silent legacy
nourished and infused such a line
such a close linked chain
to hold us until we could speak
until we could speak out
loud enough to hear ourselves
loud enough to hear ourselves
and believe our own words….

—Christine Craig from "Poem"

Throughout its growth the untiring effort, the unflagging
enthusiasm, the sacrificial contribution of time, effort, and cash
earnings of the black woman have been the most significant
factors, without which the modern Negro church would have
no history worth the writing….

—Mary McLeod Bethune

81

To study Black women of any period and in any area is not easy. No one has ever insisted on the importance of the words of Black women…So much misinformation, even mythology about early Black women writers, gets repeated without question from source to source that it is particularly important and often quite revealing to check on even the most commonplace information.

—Erlene Stetson

…there have been quite a few female musicians and a lot of them we never hear about. There have been women who have played this music as far back as Lil Armstrong in the twenties. Blanche Calloway, Cab's sister, had a band. Those kind of things aren't always well known…But things are changing now and I believe you are going to see more women in jazz (creative music) as time goes on.

—Amina Claudine Myers, jazz pianist and composer, 1986

I need to share kisses with each of you; hear
stories, and dance
I need you to drape amulets, and necklaces of your blood
around my neck,
pin ensignia clear through to my heart may I never
forget you….

—Leslie Reese from "blood around my neck"

And among the hypotheses to be tested is the idea that a black woman may indeed have designed the sphinx!

—Jeanne Noble

So we know about slavery
We write about it
We sing about it…
When do we draw the line and say,
to the best of our / ability
Come let's make modern history.

—Eveline Marius from "Let's Make History"

We were standing on the deck
of the New World, before maps….

—Rita Dove from "Mississippi"

When I was little I had this great mind for history. And I never really understood it until I realized that the reason I liked history is that I always reduced it to domestic activity. History was what people did. It was organized along the lines of who said what and who did what, not really unlike how the society in which I grew up was organized. The idea that things are impersonal occurrences is very alien to me.

—Jamaica Kincaid

hold the reflections of the past so
we will never go that way again
        —Johari M. Amini from "Story for the Remainder"

We are a complicated people as is our way of relating. I know
one thing for sure and that is that the exchange and sorting out
of herstories, much like our foremothers' oral tradition, are
essential.
        —Eleanor Johnson, Black feminist therapist

i come to claim my blood ties
        —Amina Baraka from "Soweto Song"

From my own readings on Africa and my research among the
Yoruba in Nigeria and other parts of West Africa, it appears…
in precolonial times women were conspicuous in high places.
They were queen-mothers; queen-sisters; princesses; chiefs;
and holders of other offices in towns and villages; occasional
warriors; and in one well known case, that of the Lovedu, the
supreme monarch.
        —Niara Sudarkasa

To Home

Living is worthless for one without a home.
—Ethiopian proverb

I do want to live
want to love
some woman
who might know
when the pain is on me
that I need the blues
and a bottle of everlasting spirit
to take me
from the violence
of this stolen land
home
home
home

—Stephanie Byrd from "1980"

America is our country—the only country we know. Sure,
there's good and bad people there, the same as anywhere.
But it's the ignoramuses that makes the trouble.
—Millie "Ma" Sanders, unsung World War II heroine who
was a secret link between Manila captives and MacArthur.
She hid code messages in her lemon meringue pies.

Ogoli bu uno.

Woman is the maker of home.

—Nigerian saying

a place of our own.
a row where we are known,
where hope, anguish, sweat,
have grown solid around us....
—Aneb Kgositsile from "Osage Avenue, Philadelphia,
May 13, 1985"

A Home where we are unable to voice our criticisms is not a genuine Home. Nor is a genuine Home one where you assimilate, integrate and disappear. For being invisible is the same as not being at Home. Not being at Home enough to be precisely who you are without any denials of language or culture.
—from the Introduction to *Charting the Journey*

Charity begins at home, and those that provide not for their own, are worse than infidels.
—Maria Stewart, 19th century

One thing more. I have looked over this delegation, and I wonder if you cherish the word "democracy." I say to you it means something to be free. It means a great deal. I do not think you have ever read or have ever heard of a Negro man or a Negro woman that has ever been a traitor to the United States of America...We belong to America.

—Moranda Smith (1915 - 1950), first woman to serve as Regional Director for an International labor union in the South, speaking at Final Proceedings of the 9th Constitutional Convention of the CIO, October 15, 1947.

i
be / long where
no woman goes begging.

—Leslie Reese from "Introduction"

It has been in the arena of the home that...a Black mother can actively fight racism and sexism; she can show she is a good woman by being an understanding one; she can demonstrate her toughness by exercising discipline about housework and homework; and she can relax enough to be an example of how a good-natured attitude can refresh what may otherwise be gloomy conditions. In the space of her home, a Black mother has often been an effective activist.

—Mary C. Lewis

To Our Sense of Humor

Oh big fat woman
with the meat shaking on her bones
Every time she shimmies
a skinny woman leaves her home
    —recorded by Sara Martin in 1923 from "Blind Man Blues"

Diahann Carroll,…the first black woman to star in a dramatic
network series of her own, gave this rebuttal to those who
complained that her TV show, "Julia", was not a real reflection
of Negro life: "Okay, name me one television show that's a real
reflection of *white* life!"

George Gershwin knew a great deal, he studied a great deal,
but I have been black longer than he has. I had a lot of fun
saying that. I was black all day and he wasn't. No imitator can
be as close to a thing as one who is the source.

                                                            —Eva Jessye

Do not argue with a fool for people will not be able to tell
between the two of you.

                                                            —Ibo proverb

I been cleaning up a lady porch and she tell me to tell anybody what come there that she ain't home.

A lady come and ask for her, and I tell her, "She say anybody come here, tell 'em 'I ain't home.' If you don't believe she here, look in the bedroom."

—Sylvia Cannon, ex-bondswoman, age 85 in 1937.

Now, you know that Moynihan who wrote about Black matriarchal society, knows as much about a Black family as a horse knows about New Year's.

—Fannie Lou Hamer

A young WAAC came on stage to do a comic monologue,… about the clothing she was issued and about orders telling her when to wear them. Suddenly, she began to take her clothes off, reciting a funny line with each item…off came an enlisted man's overcoat, a utility coat, a WAAC overcoat, a suit jacket, a suit skirt, a shirt, a fatigue dress, a pair of fatigue pants, a WAAC slip and a WAAC bra, leaving her, back to the audience, in only an issue girdle, so far as I could see. She paused to look over her shoulder,…and as she reached to pull off the girdle, I closed my eyes. When I heard the applause,…there she stood…:in a nearly nothing white bathing suit. She asked me later if I had not trusted her not to let me down. I told her that sometimes I would rather be let down than be frightened to death.

—Charity Adams Early, a captain in Company 8, Des Moines, Iowa, 1943.

There is not reason for blind people to have race prejudice.
—Lyda Merrick, founder of *The Negro Braille Magazine*
(now *The Merrick/Washington Magazine for the Blind*) in 1952.
It was the only national publication for sightless Blacks.

There ain't nothin' an ol' man can do but bring me a message
from a young one.

—Jackie "Moms" Mabley

I was the only dark person...in my family,...Somebody has to
be the fairest, and somebody has to be the darkest...I forgot
that we had a little blond boy; he was the fairest...and my
mother liked dressing us alike. When she took us out, she used
to say...to us, "Come on, children, let's go out and drive the
white folks crazy." And we did! Because they looked at this
little black girl and this little blond boy dressed absolutely,
totally alike. Oh, God!

—Dorothy West, novelist

when Eve
had that craving
for snake / meat
she shouldn't have
changed her mind
and settled for fruit

—Isetta Crawford Rawls from "Genesis One"

When I ran for D.C. City Council one of the reporters who interviewed me mentioned that my problem was that I was always considered to be on the Left. I said, "Well, I know that people have said I was left, and I agreed with them that yeah, I had been left out and left behind and left over.

—Josephine Butler, an early labor organizer and health educator, age 65. Founder of the D.C. Statehood Party.

De yam good?

Old lady, get yuh nails outta meh yam!
Ah mad tuh make yuh buy it now yuh damage it so bad

Dis yam look like de one dat did come off ah de ark
She brother in de Botanical Gardens up dey by Queens Park
Tourists with dey camera comin' from all over de worl'
takin' pictures dey never hear any yam could be dat ole
Ah have a crutch an' a rocking-chair someone give meh fuh free
If ah did know ah would ah bring dem an'
leave dem here fuh she

—Amryl Johnson from "Granny in de Market Place"

"Sojourner Squelches a Squawker"

It was a pleasantly warm evening in Cincinnati, in the year 1853, and the lecture hall was thronged with people who had come to hear the famous platform speaker, Sojourner Truth, expound on her favorite subject, the Abolitionist movement. When she had finished her lecture, a Southerner who was in full accord with the concept of slavery, approached her, and sneering, commented, "You were wrong in everything you said. Why, without slavery, the Negroes would starve to death. They were *made to* be slaves. As far as I am concerned, you made no more impression than a flea- bite."

"I am sorry to hear that," replied Sojourner Truth sweetly, "but perhaps, with God's help, I can keep you scratching!"

You can have all the intelligence in the world and don't have enough stamina. I have seen some very bright, bright women who do not have the stamina for husbands.

—Charleszetta Waddles

White man stop lynching and burning
This black race trying to thin it;
for if you go to heaven or hell,
you will find some Negroes in it.
—Lena Mason, 1864 - 1924, evangelist and poet
who lectured and preached throughout the
East and Midwest for more than 25 years

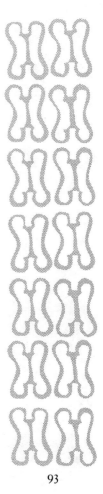

One month one of our colleagues broke a bed pan, and she is a very prominent person today. We all went down to sign for our money and we would say to each other "How much you got this month?" Some would say 5 shillings, some would say 10 shillings and, this day we asked her "Tell me how much you got?" She said, "My dear I drew my breath."
—Ruth Nita Barrow, nursing educator

It is interesting to speculate how it developed that in two of the most anti- feminist institutions, the church and the law court, the men are wearing the dresses.
—Florynce Kennedy

Ky'okujwarira ekibunu ojwarira akanwa.

Cover your mouth rather than your buttocks.
—Kigezi proverb, southwest Uganda

…trying to go through life without friendship is like milking a bear to get cream for your morning coffee. It is a whole lot of trouble, and then not worth much after you get it.

—Zora Neale Hurston

There's no sweeter cabbage
anywhere in town
You can have it boiled
until it's nice and brown
Gave some to the parson
and he shook with glee
He took up collection
gave it all to me
Gave it to a corn doctor
to fix my feet
Every time he sees me
he wants to eat
Gave some to the jailor
who turned the key on me
When I got through feeding him
he said gal you're free

—recorded by Maggie Jones, blues singer,
from "Anybody Here Want To Try My Cabbage", 1924

...and that's why it really tickled me when you talk about integration. Because I'm very black, but I remember some of my aunts was as white as anybody here—and blue-eyed and some green-eyed—and my grandfather didn't do it, you know.
—Fannie Lou Hamer

I don't care how you tried
The secret you cannot hide:
I know why you black your face,
To rank in wit like my race.
—Bettiola Heloise Fortson, born 1890
in Hopkinsville, KY. Actress, dramatic reader,
poet and suffragette, from "Found Out", 1915

I think men should be made to sell sanitary napkins on TV...We can't talk about things that are natural because they belong to women. This is stupid.
—Bertice Berry

But Black 'oman cunni' sah!
Is how dem ginal soh!
Look how long dem liberated
And de man dem never know!
—Louise Bennett, whose poetry popularized the use of
Jamaican Creole dialect. From "Jamaican 'Oman"

(Of women doctors):
Fortunate are the men who marry these women from an economic standpoint at least. They are blessed in a threefold measure, in that they take unto themselves a wife, a trained nurse, and a doctor. Unfortunate, however, is the woman physician who finds herself unevenly yoked; for such a companion will prove to be a millstone hanged around her neck. But the medically educated women are generally good diagnosticians in this direction also.

> —Dr. Susan Smith McKinney Steward, mid-to-late 1890's

I am colored but I offer nothing in the way of extenuating circumstances except the fact that I am the only Negro in the United States whose grandfather on the mother's side was not an Indian chief.

> —Zora Neale Hurston

(To a chastiser who commented that she couldn't get to heaven with smoke on her breath): Yes, chile, but when I goes to heaven I 'spects to leave my breff behind.

> —Sojourner Truth, comment c. 1879

To Our Identities

The mere fact that *your* society tells you that your sleeping
with a man makes you a "straight" womin and not a Lesbian is
about as valid as the crap that same society puts out when it
says that because you are Black you must live in the ghetto or/
and because you are female you should remain chained to the
bedroom and the scrub bucket for all of your natural life.

—Anita Cornwell

Een neger ben ik
tot in mijn zielGdraag ik
de kleur van mijn voorvaderen
de winti's, de Gadoe's ben ik
Ik been de kromanti, de apoekoe
de vodoe, de luangoe….

A black I am
even in my soul I bear
the color of my forebears
the wintis, the Gaddoes I am
I am the cromanti, the apookoo
the voodoo, the luangoo….

—Yvone Mechtelli Tjin-a-Sie from "Poem"

...stop using the word "Negro." The word is a misnomer from every point of view. It does not represent a country or anything else except one single, solitary color...We are the only human beings in the world with 57 variety of complexions who are classed together as a single racial unit.

—Mary Church Terrell

There's an expression in Puerto Rico.
" ¿Y tu abuela a dónde está?" That means if you call me nigger, what about your grandmother? Where is she and who is she? Or your mother, or your father.

—Cenen

It is time to break down the stereotype that black women can only sprint and dance.

—Tina Sloan Green, lacrosse and field hockey, U.S. Women's Lacrosse Team, 1968- 1972.

Why must it be assumed that we necessarily have to get our images of ourselves through our contacts with white Americans, when we have each other (blacks) with whom to identify?

—Lena Wright Myers

…black women are more often visualized in mainstream American culture—most prominently as fashion models or as performers in music videos—than they are allowed to speak their own words, or speak about their own condition….

—Michele Wallace

…so you see it
and here I stand black and female
bright black on the edge of this white world
and I will not blend in
nor will I fade into the midget shades
peopling your dream.

—Claire Harris from "Policeman Cleared
in Jay-Walking Case"

Yo no soy una mulatta. Yo soy una mujer negra,
y orgullosa soy una mujer negra,….
I am not a mulatto, but a Black woman,
and I am proud to be Black.

—Assata Shakur

You never find yourself until you face the truth.

—Pearl Bailey

I wonder that every colored person is not a misanthrope.
Surely we have everything to make us hate mankind.
—Charlotte Forten Grimké, written in her diary,
September 12, 1855.

If being a lesbian is not about accepting a wider range of
expression for what it means to be a woman in this world, then
I am ready to find, define, and develop a new term.
—Sabrina Sojourner

I call up my names: Woman who has been born in the arms of
a woman and welcomed home. I shout truth teller, silence
breaker, life embracer, death no longer fearing, woman re-
united with her child self. I sing woman who is daughter,
sister, lover and mother to herself. I hum woman planter,
gatherer, healer. I drum woman warrior, siren, woman who
stands firmly on her feet, woman who reaches inward to her
center and outward to stars. I am woman who is child no
longer, woman who is making herself sane, whole.
—Andrea R. Canaan

i got some Guinee in me.
I got some Ghana in me,
I got some Zairewah blood
I got some people in me,
Dahomey in me, Uganda in me,
South African blood, i got some people in me.
                    —Abbey Lincoln from "People in Me"

I am I

See me
Perceive me

But I
Shall name

My self.
          —Maud Sulter

Black women are not an exotic group who epitomize exploitation and oppression—we do not have, necessarily, a greater
insight into oppression.
                              —Kum-Kum Bhavnani

So I said, "Now, see there," in a very patient voice. "Just because I'm wearing my Super-Dyke sweatshirt, you think I'm a lesbian." I said, "I guess if I were wearing a string of pearls, you'd think I was an oyster."

—Florynce Kennedy

…and instead of looking into the mirror each morning asking, "Mirror, mirror on the wall, am I the fairest one of all?," we should begin to ask, "Mirror, mirror on the wall, am I fooling my Black self at all?"

—Dr. Frances Cress Welsing

We reject pedestals, queenhood, and walking ten paces behind. To be recognized as human, levelly human, is enough.

—Combahee River Collective

Something used by someone else carries a history with it. A piece of cloth, a platter, a cut-glass pitcher, a recipe.

A history and a spirit. You want to know when it was used. And how. And what it wants from you.

Passing demands you keep that knowledge to yourself.

—Michelle Cliff

The stuff of my being is matter, ever changing, ever moving, but never lost; so what need of denominations and creeds to deny myself the comfort of all my fellow men? The wide belt of the universe has no need for finger-rings. I am one with the infinite and need no other assurance.

—Zora Neale Hurston

I'm a Black woman…
Knowing the smell of lies
as the whole world
sits in my belly.

—Elouise Loftin from "Sunni's Unveiling"

I have always been just me, with no frame of reference to anything beyond myself.

—Bessie Head

Another empowering act has been to take charge of defining my group, of naming myself. Naming oneself, defining oneself and thereby taking the power to define out of the hands of those who wield that power over you, is an important act of empowerment…The act of self-definition thus makes clear our worth and entitlement, and sets forth our view of ourselves as one which will have to be reckoned with.

—Judy Scales-Trent

103

you know the passport forms
or even some job applications noo-a-days?
well, there's nowhere to write
Celtic-Afro-Caribbean...

Whit is an Afro-Scot anyway?
mibbe she can dance a reel and a salsa....
—Jackie Kay from "Kail and Callaloo"

...being "too learned," being too intellectual, meant that one
risked being seen as weird, strange, and possibly even mad.
—bell hooks

Similarity is not the same thing as identity.
—Ibo proverb

My life today is very peaceful. I'm a Sunni Muslim and as
observant as I can be. I don't eat pork. I've made pilgrimage. I
acknowledge the oneness of God. I pray. I contribute to
charity. I fast. And I work hard—I work until I can't see.
—Betty Shabazz, 1992

I'm a travellin woman
I got a travellin mind.
I'm gonna buy me a ticket
and ease on down the line
                    —recorded by Clara Smith, blues singer

my name is many and in truth
without all parts i have no name at all….
                    —Adjoa Andoh from "My True Name"

No me llames
sega la erva
sino morena.

Don't say
that I am the color of wheat,
call me morena.
                    —fragment of traditional folk poem from
                        16th-century Iberian Peninsula

If I could have created myself, what would I come here as? I would come here just the way I came by happenstance; I truly would. Because I celebrate myself. I see so many strengths in being a Black woman, so many strengths in being from a working class family with a rural southern background, *so many negatives too*, for all of those things! But it gives me *Me*.

—Gloria Naylor

introduce me to a world where
I don't have to miss myself....

—Leslie Reese from "Introduction"

As important for black women, the stereotypic qualities associated with lesbian women: self-assertiveness, strength, independence, eroticism, a fighting spirit, are the very qualities associated with us, qualities that we have often times suffered for and been made to feel guilty about, because they are supposedly "manly" rather than "feminine" qualities.

—Barbara Christian

        quién soy
el guerrillero, la loca que deambula,
la medusa, la flauta china,
el sillón cálido, las algas, el cañón
guardacosta, la anguistia
la sangre de los mártires, el óvulo
de ochún sobre esta tierra

        who am I
the guerrilla, the roving madwoman,
the Medusa, a Chinese flute,
a warm chair, seaweed, the coast guard's
cannon, anguish,
the blood of the martyrs, the ovum
of ochun on this earth
                    —Nancy Morejón from "Amor, Ciudad
                        Atribuída/Love, Attributed City"

I wanted a name that had something to do with struggle, something to do with the liberation of our people. I decided on Assata
Olugbala Shakur. Assata means "She who struggles," Olugbala
means "Love for the people,"…Shakur means "the thankful."
                    —Assata Shakur

107

...it is important to look at the term *black*, because not all women of African descent identify with this term. In the United States, for example, by law, people with any measurable degree of African ancestry are considered black...In this sense, *black* symbolizes a cultural milieu, more than it does a color. On the other hand, in many Caribbean and South American societies, women of African descent vary in colors that determine legal status as well as cultural identification.

—Rosalyn Terborg-Penn

To be a Black woman...is not just to be a Black who happens to be a woman, for one discovers one's sex sometime before one discovers one's racial classification.

—Kay Lindsey

I didn't think of myself as an outsider because of my race because, for one thing, where I grew up I was the same race as almost everyone else...It is true that I noticed things that no one else seemed to notice. And I think only people who are outsiders do this.

—Jamaica Kincaid, novelist and fiction writer, born in Antigua

...what I am is a humanist before anything—before I'm a Jew, before I'm black, before I'm a woman. And my beliefs are for the human race—they don't exclude anyone. But somehow we are supposed to be *credits* to our race. The mere fact that I'm still around makes me a credit to my race, which is the human race.

—Whoopi Goldberg

...when a woman, and certainly a Black woman, won't act like a Negro, a Lady and a martyr Christian, she usually gets labeled a bitch. A woman is a bitch if she stands up for herself, speaks her mind, insists on her rights and space, is not deferential to men and would rather make a scene than die or turn the other cheek.

—Judy Simmons

Yo negra soy
Porque tenga la piel
            negra
Esclava no!

I am a black woman
because my skin is black
But a slave woman no!

—Virginia Brindis De Dalas, Uruguay
poet, from "Negro: Siempre Triste"

I embrace the brown community with respect and deep loving but with firm insistence that being myself, being different, even radically different from my mothers and fathers, sisters and brothers, is my right, my duty, my way of living a whole and sane existence, accepting responsibility and consequences of being true to myself....

—Andrea Canaan

Bisexual is a safer label than lesbian, for it posits the possibility of a relationship with a man, regardless of how infrequent or non-existent the female bisexual's relationships with men might be.

—Cheryl Clarke

To Our Intellect

Not to know is bad; not to wish to know is worse.

—Nigerian proverb

Educating one woman is educating ten, while educating one man is like burning the whole thing with paraffin.

—Councillor Rushwaya for Surugwi, Zimbabwe, 1983

We discovered that all of us, because we were "smart" had also been considered "ugly," i.e., "smart-ugly." "Smart-ugly" crystallized the way in which most of us had been forced to develop our intellects at great cost to our "social" lives. The sanctions in the Black and white communities against Black women thinkers is comparatively much higher than for white women, particularly ones from the educated middle and upper classes.

—Combahee River Collective

…no Black woman can become an intellectual without decolonizing her mind.

—bell hooks

111

Nowhere can (a) woman obtain better preparation for life than within the college walls. There are a host of young colored women who have gone out and are still going out and nobly defending the cause of higher education for the colored girl.
—Annie Pace, educator, 1909

To the degree that a society is oppressive, education is into having you suspend the exercise of your intellect.
—Florynce Kennedy

One who learns, teaches.
—Ethiopian proverb

We have rarely been encouraged and equipped to appreciate the fact that the truth works, that it releases the Spirit and that it is a joyous thing. We live in a part of the world, for example, that equates criticism with assault, that equates social responsibility with naive idealism, that defines the unrelenting pursuit of knowledge and wisdom as fanaticism.
—Toni Cade Bambara

Obwengye burya amaani.

Wisdom eats strength.
—Kigezi proverb, southwest Uganda

Here's a riddle for Our Age: when the
        sky's the limit,
   how can you tell you've gone too far?
                          —Rita Dove from "And Counting"

A good deal of time and intelligence has been invested in the
exposure of racism and horrific results on its objects…But that
well-established study should be joined with another, equally
important one: the impact of racism on those who perpetuate it.
                          —Toni Morrison

I guess my frustration in life has been that I was multitalented.
Society prepares you to deal with only one talent, so you have
to choose. Ministry is the first place where I've been able to do
it all.
        —Suzan Johnson Cook, first Black woman ever called to
                senior pastorate by an American Baptist Church
                congregation and in October 1990, the first female
                        chaplain for the NYC Police Department.

…black co-eds would perhaps be the first group to recognize
that a college education might cause alienation from the
masses of black people. Their fears are well founded.
                          —Jeanne Noble

My father objected to me going to college,...His idea of a girl was that you got married and had children. See, he was a different generation. A girl that went to college became a queer woman. She didn't act like a woman. And he didn't want to be the father of a queer girl. So he gave nothing to me going to college.

—Dr. May Edward Chinn

I am *both* Black *and* a woman...And yet I am continually asked to prioritize my consciousness; is race more important; is gender more important? Which is more severe, etc.? The fallacy lies not in struggling with the answer, in trying to figure out which is the correct answer for the group at hand, but the fallacy lies with the question itself.

—Patricia Hill Collins, 1990

Knowledge is like a garden; if it is not cultivated, it cannot be harvested.

—Guinea proverb

To be educated meant you could take your place in life.

—Ardie Clark Halyard

When I was a little girl my grandmother—who was in her early seventies—would say: "Child you're black and you are going to be a woman and I don't think you can change either one of the two. But you are bright and you have a brain. Use it to show them you are coming through."

—Shirley Chisholm

I defy anybody to tell me that I can't think because I am a female. I defy anybody to say that I can't think because of my age... I have them all laughing that you will never put me in a corner anywhere. I would build myself a round room first so that there would be no corners.

—Juanita Jewel Craft, age 73

The dread inspired by the growing intelligence of colored women has interested us almost to the point of amusement. It has given to the colored women a new sense of importance to witness how easily their emancipation and steady advancement is disturbing all classes of American people.

—Fannie Barrier Williams

USA TODAY: What is Marva Collins' method of instruction?

MARVA COLLINS: It is all about believing in yourself and not allowing people to break your spirit. It is about determination and belief in what you can do... Our creed is that society predicts but our students will determine.

Wha' yu no know oler dan yu.

What you do not know is older than you.

—Jamaican proverb

Ugi ni kihooto.

Knowledge is power.

—Kikuyu proverb

And grandma would just look at me and ask, are we *pretending* not to know today?" The premise being that colored people on the planet earth really know everything there is to know. And if one is not coming to grips with the knowledge, it must mean that one is either scared or pretending to be stupid.

—Toni Cade Bambara

A slave is still a slave if she refuses to think for herself.

—Ibo proverb

Kuira ti kurita.

To be black is not to be stupid.

—Kikuyu proverb

...I realized that while my degrees and money might in fact protect me to a certain point, they couldn't protect me all the way. A reformist posture towards society that says that gender, or social class, is the only thing that we need to address, that does not take into account the workings of race, is not enough for me; it is a partial solution.

—Patricia Hill Collins

Too much discussion means a quarrel.

—Ivory Coast proverb

I grant you that intellectual development, with the self-reliance and capacity for earning a livelihood which it gives, renders woman less dependent on the marriage relation for physical support (which, by the way, does not always accompany it). Neither is she compelled to look to sexual love as the one sensation capable of giving tone and relish, movement and vim to the life she leads.

—Anna Julia Cooper

Ny teny marina hoatra ny fia-pary,
ka ny lava aza tsy lany hamamiana.

Truth is like sugar cane: even if you
chew it for a long time, it is still sweet.

—Malagasy proverb

Truth burns up error.

—Sojourner Truth, comment c. 1882

To remove ignorance is an important branch of benevolence.
—Ann Plato

Contradiction or even apparent contradiction could be called
the other name of truth.

—Bessie Head

To Joy

I have reversed the saying of
Troubles are like Babies
the more you nurse them
the bigger They grow
so I have nursed the joys

—Juanita Harrison

Whenever I play I throw myself away. It doesn't matter where
I am. I close my eyes and leave this earth.
—Mary Lou Williams, jazz pianist

What a people—we make something out of nothing and revel
in its simple delicacy!

—Carol Talbot

Success is getting what you want and happiness is wanting
what you get.

—Ibo proverb

With life I am on the attack, restlessly ferreting out each
pleasure, foraging for answers, wringing from it even the pain.
I ransack life, hunt it down. I am the hungry peasants storming
the palace gates. I will have my share. No matter how it tastes.

—Marita Golden

Basket full, 'ooman laugh.

—Jamaican proverb

I do not think that there is anything quite as painful as not
being able to laugh; sometimes.

—Bessie Head

we lock eyes
laugh the bottom out of hell,
gnash teeth in kisses,
trade skins.

—Rikki Lights from "Lovers"

Anticipate the good so that you may enjoy it.

—Ethiopian proverb

…choosing to love another Black woman is really not about being anti-male at all but participating in a kind of celebratory rejoicing in one's womanness.

—bell hooks

Our most memorable days are marked by an absence of control.
—Patricia Smith from "Wallenda"

Let us begin to recognize the wonderful continuum involved in being unabashedly and excitingly and intensely female. Let us affirm this woman in the world and in ourselves.
—Sabrina Sojourner

I struggle to live for the beauty of a pansy
for a little black baby's song
for my lover's laugh
I struggle for the blaze of pink
across the evening sky
for some bar-b-cue ribs
I struggle for life and the pursuit of its happiness
I struggle to fill my house
        with joy

—Stephanie Byrd from "Every Day"

Everybody has their place of just absolute brilliance and I *want* that. I want everybody to be in that place of self-knowledge and ecstasy, cause that means we're all free.

—Rachel Bagby

so the hell with what your mama told you,
dance in the worst way.
dance upside down,
on your hair, on your knees,
dance tight and illegal,
dance on the rule book, sister....

—Patricia Smith from "Nawlins Tango"

Such as I am, I am a precious gift....

—Zora Neale Hurston

My statement is simple. It says: "Live! Get your thing together, your ass off the ground and do it! Go past the bullshit in this life, the bullshit in the system, on your job, and do you! Get off on you because that is the best getting off of all.

—Nona Hendryx, singer

Ukupha yikuzibekela.

Giving is storing up for oneself.

—Ndebele proverb

I'm having a good time,
Please don't blame me,
I'm knocking myself out
Don't try to tame me
Let me have my fun,
I've got to have my fling,
Some folks say I'm blowing my top
Talk don't mean a thing,…

—Alberta Hunter, blueswoman, originally entitled
"I'm Having A Gay Time" written in 1949

The more you praise and celebrate your life, the more there is in life to celebrate.

—Oprah Winfrey, entertainer

let us dance and move in a circle
and when it has been broken
let there be only smiles for what we had

—Mae Jackson from "For The Count"

To Our Kids

(Advice to children on crossing the street):
Damn the lights. Watch the cars. The lights ain't never killed nobody.
> —Jackie "Moms" Mabley (c. 1894 - 1975), comedienne

I tell my children. Never use the words, "I can't." Say, "I'll try."
> —Ruby Middleton Forsythe

Omwana ye yeerindwa ennyo.

A child is to be treated very carefully.
> —Luganda proverb

O Children of no childhood
murdered as a policy of state,
we bury your slender coffins in lakes of tears,
but our fists pound the air like oaths.
> —Aneb Kgositsile from "South Africa Poem"

Ny ankizy no manao tsingeringerina ka ny lehibe no fanina.

The children dance and the grown people get dizzy.

—Malagasy proverb

Don't let anybody make you feel like your child is your greatest burden, that because you had a child, life is over for you. That's garbage. Understand that we are in a state of war. And sisters, you're going to have to put that baby on your back and keep moving.

—Sister Souljah, rap vocalist

...no-one can abandon children, you just cannot abandon human life. If you haven't got your real mother concentrating on you, someone has to.

—Bessie Head

When a woman is hungry, she says, "Roast something for the children that they may eat."

—Ashanti proverb

In my daughter's name
I bless your child with the mother she has
with a future of warriors and growing fire.

> —Audre Lorde from "Dear Toni
> Instead of a Letter of Congratulation
> Upon Your Book and Your Daughter Whom You
> Say You Are Raising To Be a Correct Little Sister"

Children know this: they are
the trailings of gods. Their eyes
hold nothing at birth then fill slowly
with the myth of ourselves.

> —Rita Dove from "The Breathing, The Endless News"

An illegitimate child is one who is not wanted, and must be
cast away or rejected...Our experiences have proved that we
must accept those whom we have borne to ensure our immor-
tality as a people. In view of this, we can say that we blacks
don't have any illegitimate children.

> —Dr. Alyce C. Gullattee, psychiatrist

Pikni da po' pipple riches.

Children are poor people's riches.

> —Creole proverb, British Honduras

She formed a space in me as deep
and calm as jungle halls this child
who would inherit fable
in her genius of the ancestors....
—Claire Harris from "this was the child I dreamt"

The child who raises its arms will be embraced.
—Yoruba proverb

In every culture, it is true that youth is unencumbered by inhibitions. In South Africa, children are uninhibited even by war. The absence of inhibition in these children, however, is not equivalent to the usual naivete that is the basis of most children's fearlessness. For naivete is the product of an innocent ignorance of the consequences of one's actions. And these children, though they may be innocent, know all too well the consequences of their actions.
—Angela Y. Davis

Hit a child and quarrel with its mother.
—Hausa Proverb

A great tragedy
has occurred.
there are no more
"great american heroes"
to look to, children;
only the ever-present
Hero within yourselves.
and within
your people.

—Linda Cousins from "The Tragedy"

…they're not going to give us what *they* have, the birth control people. They just want us to be a poor version of them, only without our children and our faith in God and our tasty fried food, or anything.

—anonymous Georgia woman telling how she felt about family planning in the 1960's

Ne gw'ozadde: akukubira ennoma n'ozina.

Even your child might beat the drum for you while you dance.

—Luganda proverb

To Our Liberation and Unity

In black women's liberation we don't want to be equal with men, just like in black liberation we're not fighting to be equal with the white man. We're fighting for the right to be different and not be punished for it.

—Margaret Wright, activist, 1970

The essence of a free life is being able to choose the style of living you prefer free from exclusion and without the compulsion of conformity or law.

—Eleanor Holmes Norton, equal rights activist, born 1937. Commencement Address, Barnard College, NY, June 6, 1972.

We need women who will not follow blindly a party because of its name, women who will break away from any party that does not stand for absolute equality of opportunity for each and every human being. We should insist that the Negro women get their rightful share of all public offices,....

—Mrs. Robert M. Patterson, Socialist candidate for the General Assembly in Philadelphia, PA, in the 1920's

129

When we speak of peace, we must also speak of freedom.
—Angela Y. Davis

Otakaraaragakwo tomutakira njara.

Don't talk of hunger to one who never missed a meal.
—Kizegi proverb, southwest Uganda

I ain't gonna do any mo' hoeing
I ain't gonna pick any mo' berries...
the sun gonna shine for me
and go down when I sez so....
—Karen Mitchell from "Anna, After Slavery"

A govenrment which can protect and defend its citizens from
wrong and outrage and does not is vicious. A governemnt
which would do it and cannot is weak; and where human life is
insecure through either weakness or viciousness in the admin-
istration of law, there must be a lack of justice and where there
is wanting, nothing can make up the deficiency.
—Frances E. W. Harper

Iri gukura iriagwo iguku ni aka.

When a bull becomes old, its hump is eaten by women.
(The old order will eventually change.)

—Gikuyu proverb

I often say to people that I have a right to shout more than
some folks; I have been bought twice, and set free twice, and so
I feel I have a good right to shout. Hallelujah!

—Amanda Berry Smith, itinerant
preacher, born in Maryland in 1837

…it is the women of a country who help to mold its character,
and to influence if not determine its destiny….

—Frances E. W. Harper, 19th century

Olwo waikala noigiliza olileniwa okwase

Constant dripping wears away a stone.

—Haya proverb

Literacy means liberation.

—Septima P. Clark

A democracy cannot long endure with the head of a God and the tail of a demon.

> —Josephine Silone Yates, 1852 - 1912, educator, writer; a president of the National Association of Colored Women

The stakes…are too high for government to be a spectator sport.

> —Barbara Jordan, Commencement address, Harvard University, June 16, 1977

South Africa is the only country in the world where racism is a declared policy of the state. One wonders what the world understands by this statement. For South African black people it is a loaded statement which explodes on their heads every minute of their lives.

> —Ruth Mompati

…if we focus exclusively on sexism and racism we remain mired in the myths we are trying to dissipate.

> —Elizabeth Fox-Genovese

The stone in the water does not know how hot the hill is, parched by the sun.

> —Nigerian proverb

Those who consider themselves to be revolutionary must begin to deal with other revolutionaries as equals. And so far as I know, revolutionaries are not determined by sex.

—Frances Beal

She who tells the truth is not well liked.

—Bambara proverb

If we are not afraid to adopt a revolutionary stance—if, indeed, we wish to be radical in our quest for change— then we must get to the root of our oppression. After all, *radical* simply means "grasping things at the root."

—Angela Y. Davis

Now that you have touched the women, you have struck a rock, you have dislodged a boulder, and you will be crushed.

—chant by South African women during the 1956 campaign against pass laws.

I have always felt it was a handicap for oppressed peoples to depend so largely upon a leader, because unfortunately in our culture, the charismatic leader usually becomes a leader because he has found a spot in the public limelight...There is also the danger in our culture that because a person is called upon to give public statements and is acclaimed by the establishment, such a person gets to the point of believing that he *is* the movement. Such people get so involved with playing the game of being important that they don't exhaust themselves and their time, and they do the work of actually organizing people.

—Ella Baker

War ends nothing.

—Mongo proverb, Zaire

It is our duty to fight for our freedom.
It is our duty to win.
We must love each other and support each other.
We have nothing to lose but our chains

—Assata Shakur

True leaders have to be totally free.

—Shirley Chisholm

You got to stop lookin' at my black skin and I got to stop lookin' at yo' black heart. I want to clear up yo' black heart and I want you to clear up in yo' mind about my black skin and we'll get together as a human race. Instead of that you can just stand there and count prejudice. Up to the thousands. You can just look at it.

—Onnie Lee Logan

I don't believe in segregation. And I refuse to segregate myself because that's the only way I can say to the other fellow, "Don't you segregate me."

—Juanita Jewel Craft, age 73

Someone else's legs do you no good in traveling.

—Nigerian proverb

MARGARET WALKER: Do you want to split the world straight down the middle?

NIKKI GIOVANNI: I don't want to split the world, it's split already. And if that's the way it is, then I want my side to come out number one.

—a dialogue from *A Poetic Equation*

Ef women want any rights more'n dey's got, why don't dey jes' *take 'em*, and not be talkin' about it.
—Sojourner Truth, comment c. 1863

Like treating a cancer, we must burn the diseased tissues of society's thinking without killing off the live creature.
—Lauretta Ngcobo

I guess the secret of my youth is struggle.
—Miriam Makeba, South African singer and activist
(upon turning age 50 in 1982)

A revolution cannot change your status, even though you change hands for government. You still retain the same status that you had previously because you have not done anything about your liberation. Black people must liberate themselves before they can talk about revolution.
—Dara Abubakari (Virginia E. Y. Collins)

Andu matari ndundu mahuragwo na njuguma imwe.

People who have no unity are conquered with one club (weapon).
—Gikuyu proverb

We exist as women who are black who are feminists, each stranded for the moment, working independently because there is not yet an environment in this society remotely congenial to our struggle— because, being on the bottom, we would have to do what no one else has done: we would have to fight the world.

—Michele Wallace

For me, it's a concept of militance that means that you don't keep working *about* something, you work *on* it...a militant attack for me means a direct attack... militant doesn't mean rhetoric or threats.

—Dorothy Height

I went to work at a village school as head of the home economics department...We were supposed to teach a European diet—a three-course meal that even a teacher couldn't afford. We used electricity and gas to cook. So I took the students out and we built a fireplace and collected vegetables and made our own recipes based on local foods. The inspectress didn't like it and she was so angry that she made my life very tough.

—Sithembiso Nyoni

137

You can dramatize war but we don't yet know how to dramatize peace.

        —Dr. Zelma Watson George

Wannko bi a wose yannko

Those who are not involved in a battle are always skeptical about the dangers of the front.

        —Yoruba proverb

Everyone else is represented in Washington by a rich and powerful lobby, it seems. But there is no lobby for the people.

        —Shirley Chisholm

...I think that the answer to violence is a response.

        —Nikki Giovanni

Habran mayno oo dhaqanka, waan u hawl gelaynaa
Hurdow toos! Hurdow toos!

We shall not hold back, we shall toil for our heritage.
Awake, you who are asleep! Awake, you who are asleep!

        —Somali language

Black people are the only segment in American society that is defined by its weakest elements. Every other segment is defined by its highest achievement. We have to turn that around.
—Jewell Jackson McCabe

I have ceased a long time ago to exist as an individual…The ideals, the political goals that I stand for, those are the ideals and goals of the people in this country…When they send me into exile, it's not me as an individual they are sending…What I stand for is what they want to banish. I couldn't think of a greater honor.
—Winnie Mandela, 1990

Kahunu getaga kahutu gakoroku (kagugunyi).

The person who has eaten enough, calls the one who is hungry greedy.
—Gikuyu proverb

What is the meaning of participation in a society that doesn't allow participation? You can encourage women to participate but that is not the issue. The issue is to create a society where everyone participates as equals.
—Sithembiso Nyoni

A single bracelet does not jingle.

—Congo proverb

For Nigerian women the path to liberation is the same as for any oppressed group. In the first stage, individuals start thinking and saying the unthinkable, challenging the ideas which have traditionally dominated the relationship between men and women. The second stage is reached when the more intelligent and sensitive members of society start to listen to what is being said. Gradually, more and more people recognize the truth and begin to act on it.

—Taiwo Ajai

If we understand that we are talking about a struggle that is hundreds of years old, then we must acknowledge a continuance: that to be Black women is to move forward the struggle for the kind of space in this society that will make sense for our people.

—Bernice J. Reagon

…right to life is not inherent, but is by grace of…an enemy. I think that those who so loudly proclaim perfect freedom call out triumphantly before being out of the difficulty.

—Mary Shadd Cary, 1872

We decided that, if the gun is what the South African regime has used to rule us, it will have to be the gun that breaks that rule.
—Ruth Mompati, a leader and member of the African National Congress (ANC)

Homophobia divides black people as political allies, it cuts off political growth, stifles revolution, and perpetuates patriarchal domination.
—Cheryl Clarke

What are we talking about when we speak of revolution if not a free society made up of whole individuals?
—Toni Cade

In Africa, as well as in the diaspora, the black women engaged in research on the black woman are involved in a process of liberation, as well as in a scholarly endeavor, since research, being essentially a product of the power structure, has sometimes been used as a tool of domination.
—Filomina Chioma Steady, anthropologist

To Love

Love is such a powerful force. It's there for everyone to embrace—that kind of unconditional love for all of humankind. That is the kind of love that impels people to go into the community and try to change conditions for others, to take risks for what they believe in.

—Coretta Scott King

I love you for your brownness,
And the rounded darkness of your breast,
I love you for the breaking sadness in your voice
And shadows where your wayward eyelids rest.

—Gwendolyn B. Bennett from "To A Dark Girl"

I have known the joy and pain of deep friendship. I have served and been served. I have made some good enemies for which I am not a bit sorry. I have loved unselfishly, and I have fondled hatred with the red-hot tongs of Hell. That's living.

—Zora Neale Hurston

Much growth is stunted by too careful prodding,
Too eager tenderness.
The things we love we have to learn to leave alone.
—Naomi Long Madgett from "Woman With Flower"

Ruendo rutiri guoya

Love has no fear.

—Gikuyu proverb

…in a White supremacist country, the Black person who is
most threatening is the one who loves Blackness, who loves the
embodiment of Blackness, the mark of Blackness on the skin,
in the body.

—bell hooks

Kwenda ti kwendithio

Love cannot be forced.

—Gikuyu proverb

Afro-American women have repeatedly manifested their love, their perseverance, their vision, their faith, their loyalty, their perceptivity, and an uncanny ability to compromise without being compromised.

—Sylvia Lyons Render, specialist in
African American history and culture

…you will not find the law of love shut out from the affairs of men after the feminine half of the world's truth is completed.
—Anna Julia Cooper

"understand this.
my basis
for loving wimmin
is my love for
five younger sisters, my
momma, and myself…."

—doris davenport from "Sisterhood"

Talking with one another is loving one another.
—Kenyan proverb

you are my treasure
and I am yourn
and in the life
a treasure
is rare to find
rarer to keep
I say
are you my treasure
repeat you are my treasure
and I yourn

—Stephanie Byrd from "Hunt"

how is it possible
that women could
love each other so?
and we said: it was possible
cuz it happened
in so many conversations
so many attempts
to understand ourselves....

—Nubia Kai from "Sisters"

The women that we love!
Their slit-eyed ways
Of telling us to mind, pop-eyed dismays.
We need these folks, each one of them. We do.
                    —Elizabeth Alexander from "Letter: Blues"

Love, I find, is like singing. Everybody can do enough to
satisfy themselves, though it may not impress the neighbors as
being very much.

                    —Zora Neale Hurston

Who knows better than we,
With the dark, dark bodies,
What it means
When April comes a-laughing and a-weeping
Once again
At our hearts?

                    —Angelina Weld Grimké from "At April"

Ou okunda takushereka kigambo.

One who loves you does not spare you the truth.
                    —Kigezi proverb, southwest Uganda

What is holy and infinite
seems neither to be grass
nor cement
but the acts of love
which hallow them.

—Adrienne Ingrum from "Loomit"

…all of us would do well to stop fighting each other for our
space at the bottom, because there ain't no more room. We
have spent so much time hating ourselves. Time to love
ourselves. And that…is the final resistance.

—Cheryl Clarke

You will not swallow me or absorb me:
I have grown too lean for that.
I am selfish, I am cruel,
     I am love.

—Pinkie Gordon Lane from "On Being Head
of the English Department"

To Our Mommas

Even today when we extol the virtues of our mamas, most often it's a litany of hard work, of what she did without and what she gave—never what she took or expected or demanded as her due.
                                        —Marcia Ann Gillespie, writer and editor

isi nmili

the source of the spring—the mother

                                                                —Ibo

We women have always been the ones to construct and piece together sanctuary and refuge for all our people—our neighborhoods, our family. When you get hurt, you go to Mama.
                                        —June Jordan

It is because our mothers, our elders, had the charge of children that they were—and remain—responsible for training them, for transmiting certain myths and beliefs, and instilling in them a spirit of submission to customs. In refusing to allow Black African civilization to be destroyed, our mothers were revolutionary.
                                        —Awa Thiam

Nyina omwana aba omubazi ogutamba enda.

Mother is the first medicine for the stomach.
                                        —Kigezi proverb, southwest Uganda

The hand that rocks the cradle rules the nation and its destiny.
                                        —South African proverb

…Her mothers taught her well to humor
those ignorant of her powers, taught her
 how to keep herself alive…
                                        —Valerie Jean from "At Full Moon"

Mi madre tuvo el canto y el pañuelo
para acunar la fe de mis entrañas,
para alzar su cabeza de reina desoída….

My mother had the handkerchief and the song
to cradle my body's deepest faith,
and hold her head high, banished queen….
                                        —Nancy Morejón from "Madre/Mother"

Mother is gold.

                                        —Yoruba proverb

149

The truth is I had the child. Look at the womb print.
                                    —Thylias Moss from "Denial"

Mothering/nurturing is a vital force and process establishing
relationships throughout the universe. Exploring and analyzing
the nature of all components involved in a nurturing activity
puts one in touch with life extending itself. This is the feminine presence. The earth is woman. Africa is a woman.
                                    —Bernice J. Reagon

Ekikwiziire kubi okihongyera nyoko.

What is difficult for you, take to your mother.
                                    —Kizegi proverb, southwest Uganda

Mothers beget children but not their heart.
                                    —Trinidad proverb

And another thing (my mother) used to say to me is, "Keep
your mouth shut and do what you want to. You don't have to
talk so much; just keep your mouth shut and go ahead and do
what you're going to do."
                                    —Mary Crutchfield Thompson

Black women as mothers and teachers consciously can teach their daughters that Black women, as the mothers of all mankind, are the alpha and the omega of women on this planet.
—Dr. Frances Cress Welsing

A mother is a mother, ye Zulus!

—Xhosa proverb

My mom always said the quickest way not to get what you want in the world is not to ask for it.
—Anna Perez, press secretary to Barbara Bush, former First Lady, 1990

My mother told me to be overeducated for everything you do. She also told me to remember always be more educated than anybody in the room. She said: "Let them say anything they want about you. But when you look around the room make sure you know more than anybody there."

—Mary Frances Berry

What my mother teaches me are the essential lessons of the quilt: that people and actions do move in multiple directions at once.
—Elsa Barkley Brown

A woman is a mother, and women are the people who are suffering most…If the government continues killing children, the women will become even more angry, and these are the people who will take up the struggle.

—Nontsikelelo Albertina Sisulu

I search my mother's face
neatly carved in obsidian
and wonder
how much of myself I owe this woman….

—Irma McClaurin from "The Power of Names"

My grandmothers are full of memories
Smelling of soap and onions and wet clay
With veins rolling roughly over quick hands
They have many clean words to say,
My grandmothers were strong.

—Margaret Walker from "Lineage"

To Our Power

talkin bout a woman
talkin bout what the old world
never thought a woman
could be, or do, or imagine
so amazed
they had to look again
they had to change definitions
—Nubia Kai from "Harriet Tubman"

One thing what makes fear is power. I don't have anything that they can take and I'm not afraid of losing nothing, 'cause you can't lose something you don't have...I never had a reputation 'cause I always been a troublemaker, so I didn't lose that.
—Cora Lee Johnson

Woman is king.

—Sotho proverb

…return to yourself.
Do not forget to
keep your powers alive.

> —Becky Birtha from "The Healing Poem"

Self-definition is intimately linked with empowerment.

> —Judy Scales-Trent

Ethiopia's queens will reign again, and her Amazons protect her shores and people. Strengthen your shaking knees, and move forward, or we will displace you and lead on to victory and to glory.

> —Amy-Jacques Garvey

Some folks talk about my power.
Some folks say I'm wild and strong.
Others say my style of living makes a man go wrong.
I'm a woman hard to handle, if you need to handle things.
Better run when I start coming.
I got thunder and it rings.

> —Abbey Lincoln, singer and composer,
> from "I Got Thunder"

Inonga iratsa.

Even the humble one kicks.
(Still waters run deep.)

—Luyia saying

The island women move through Paris
as if they had just finished inventing
their destinations. It's better
not to get in their way. And better
not look an island woman in the eye—
unless you like feeling unnecessary.
—Rita Dove from "The Island Women of Paris"

For women to put our hopes and desires into words is still a
magical and rebellious thing in spite of how common it may
seem to be. To have the freedom to push our ideas and words
further than they have in the past is a gift many women before
us have not been able to savor (and many still cannot).
—Jewelle Gomez, poet and writer

We must concentrate on what we can do and erase "can't,"
"won't" and "don't think so" from our vocabulary.
—Cardiss Collins

155

I've learned of life this bitter truth
Hope not between the crumbling walls
Of mankind's gratitude to find repose,
But rather,
Build within thy own soul
Fortresses!

> —Georgia Douglas Johnson, 1886 - 1967,
> musician, composer, poet, writer. From
> "Lessons," originally published in 1924.

The community women I worked with on projects were respected and admired for their strength and endurance. They worked hard in the cotton fields or white folks' houses, raised and supported their children, yet still found the time and energy to be involved in struggle for their people. They were typical rather than unusual.

> —Cynthia Washington, Civil rights activist

US TODAY: How does meditation improve your life?

PHYLICIA RASHAD: It is the power that leads you to your own truth. Everybody needs to be free. The main thing meditation frees you from is the idea of "do-ership," the thinking that "I am doing this." When you're free from the idea of do-ership then something else within you emerges. It is yourself.

Tumsi langa wi de wakti
Kon mek' wi sori wi eygi krakti

Too long we have been waiting
come let us show our own strength
—Gladys Waterberg from
"Meki Wi Sori Wi Eygi Krakti"

I have always felt that one great advantage of being both Black
and a woman was that I started off with nothing to lose.
—Naomi Sims

When it comes to the cause of justice, I take no prisoners and I
don't believe in compromising.
—Mary Frances Berry

Look at her face. Men fear the "tick mama." She can say what
she feels. Her yams will always be sold in the same place.
—Buchi Emecheta

Kiss (ass) til you could kick (ass).
—Creole proverb, British Honduras

It is time for Black women to move and be moved beyond myth to power!

—Marcia Ann Gillespie, writer and editor

The Black woman griot-historian must be baptised by some force outside the tradition of Western civilization and become submerged in the waters of Black women's pain, power, and potential.

—Barbara Omolade

In Mississippi two young Klansmen came in and threw trash where my secretary was registering people to vote…I walked up to one of them and jammed my finger in his chest and said, "You don't tear up anything I put together. Now get out of here!" Common sense would tell you, don't do that. I didn't think, I just acted. I was mad.

—Althea T. L. Simmons

she, the woman
marches from many paths
untying knots
sickling tied overgrowths of want

—Lindiwe Mabuza

I make this pledge to my people, the dead and the living—to all Americans, black and white. I will not retire nor will I retreat, not one inch, so long as God gives me vision to see what is happening and strength to fight for the things I know are right. For I know that my kingdom, my people's kingdom and the kingdom of all the peoples of all the world, is not beyond the skies, the moon and the stars, but right here at our feet.

—Charlotta Bass, candidate for U.S. Vice-President,
Progressive Party Convention, April 1952.

It is very good to do new things that our husbands never thought we could do.

—Regina Chamboko, builder of mud stoves, Zimbabwe, 1983

...we can be our own voices of authority.

—Elsa Barkley Brown

...the loneliness, the sense of being really, really small and limited...I have been able to delimit and control that, because I have made myself aware of other women and other people, period, on the planet besides myself. I recognize that I don't have a right, really, to feel so bad at all. That, on the contrary, I have privileges of power that I really need to be trying to use in more and more responsible ways.

—June Jordan

For it is not the color of the skin that makes the man or the woman, but the principle formed in the soul. Brilliant wit will shine, come from whence it will; and genius and talent will not hide the brightness of its lustre.

—Maria Stewart

…despite whites' misconceptions about us, they are attracted to us. I have often said that once having touched the soil of the black mother earth, they always go back to be replenished. There is truly something magic about the power of the black female.

—Alyce C. Gullatee, psychiatrist

Mon rwotgi peke.

Women have no chiefs.
(Chiefs are not chiefs to women.)

—Acholi proverb

A functioning human being is never totally without power. Wherever we have been enslaved, we have in some way given assent. We have allowed the condition to develop or persist.

—Dr. Carole A. Oglesby

Kiringiri gia aka ni rwenji rukirega.

To force a woman to do something she doesn't like is like forcing a blunt shaving-knife to shave.

—Kikuyu proverb

I remember when I was a young nurse in Barbados and there were a lot of breakages of dishes and so on in the nurses' hostel. When we went to collect our money at the end of the month everybody had to pay 2 shillings and sixpence for a plate and in those days a plate was 6 pence. So I retired to the nurses' hostel, took up a plate, went out on the steps, took a stone, broke it in 4 and when the Warden complained, I said that was the plate I paid for.

—Ruth Nita Barrow, nursing educator, Barbados

I will resist every attempt to categorize me, to place me in some caste, or to assign me to some segregated pigeonhole… No law which imprisons my body or custom which wounds my spirit can stop me.

—Pauli Murray, Civil rights lawyer and then ordained priest of Episcopal Church

…I have to make things happen through the force of my personality. Most power is illusionary and perceptual. You have to create an environment in which people perceive you as having some power.

—Carrie Saxon Perry

Ego is a killer. Humility is probably the greatest power that one can study, to understand that you didn't create anything here…I feel that if you study humility in your work, in your life, you will be studying the power of success.

—Melba Moore

All questions can't be answered through objectivity, and certainly the Black woman's power and knowing can't be understood without a knowing of her spirit and spiritual life.

—Barbara Omolade

Why, I feel so tall within—I feel as if the power of a nation is within me!

—Sojourner Truth, 1878

…we cannot do things unless we become aware of ourselves and our woman-power…If given the chance, women are the most powerful force under the sun.

—Florence de Villiers

…learn to cherish
that boisterous Black Angel that
        drives you
up one day and down another
protecting the place where your power
        rises….
                        —Audre Lorde from "For Each Of You"

earth-colored women…
your riches lie in state
and we pass by
not as mourners but as believers
as pursuers of your chariots
that have long lit the sky
                        —Nikky Finney from "Chariots"

is it too late to get back your lightning
is it too late to reconstruct your song
        blues song sister tell me
is it too late for the mother tongue in
        your womanself to insurrect
                        —Jayne Cortez from "Grinding Vibrato"

To Our Protection

It doesn't do us any good as Black people to hide what we believe is wrong because it may be perceived as a betrayal. It is an unfortunate and awful position for Black women to be in. It is interesting that people have not seen the harassment of Black women as a betrayal.

—Anita Hill

Father, Mother, Older Man, Older Woman,
Uncle, Aunt, Brother, Sister, Young Woman,
Be a hedge around her
Bruise not the flower.

—Nelcia Robinson from "Young Woman"

I think every woman owes it to herself to protect her body from careless promiscuous handling of Tom, Dick and Harry.

—Christia Daniels Adair

The world salutes
those women who grasp weapons....

—Shirley Small from "Women of Bulawayo and Others"

...for we have always been the receivers
of what is given without love or permission....

—Ai from "Fate"

Mundu muka ndoragagwo.

A woman must not be killed.

—Kikuyu proverb

Black people who were living in the South were constantly
living with violence... The major job was getting people to
understand that they had something within their power that
they could use, and it could only be used if they understood
what was happening and how group action could counter
violence even when it was perpetrated by the police or, in some
instances, the state. My basic sense of it has always been to get
people to understand that in the long run they themselves are
the only protection they have against violence or injustice.
—Ella Baker, freedom movement organizer
and founder of the Student Non-Violent Coordinating
Committee (SNCC) and the Mississippi Freedom
Democratic Party, 1964.

We need men to stop giving consent, by their silence, to rape,
to sexual abuse, to violence.

—Byllye Avery

Blacks clearly recognized that to master the language of whites was in effect to consent to be mastered by it through the white definition of caste built into the semantic/social system. Inversion therefore becomes the defensive mechanism which enables Blacks to fight linguistic, and thereby psychological, entrapment.
—Grace Sims Holt, scholar and teacher

The one doctrine of my mother's teaching which was branded upon my senses was that I should never let anyone abuse me. "I'll kill you, gal, if you don't stand up for yourself," she would say. "Fight, and if you can't fight, kick; if you can't kick, then bite."
—Cornelia, born in bondage, 1844, in Tennessee

Since black women share a negative group label imposed from the outside, they feel a need to come together for mutual protection. This "perceived need to band together in defense against domination or hostility" is one major source of cultural identity.
—Judy Scales-Trent

Do not look where you fell, but where you slipped.
—Vai proverb, Liberia

Never wound a snake, kill it.

—Harriet Tubman

To Our Self-Esteem

Cat does run away, dog does run away
Fowl does run away when you treating them bad
What happen to you?
Woman, you can run away too.
>   —Singing Francine, calypso singer,
>   from "Run Away," 1979

...self is a friend you can call
by your name and be
honest in reply.
>   —Esther Louise from "it's all in the name"

We must have a glorified womanhood that can look any man
in the face—white, red, yellow, brown, or black, and tell of the
nobility of character within black womanhood...The men ought to
get down on their knees to Negro women. They have made
possible all we have around us—church, home, school, business.
>   —Nannie H. Burroughs

A slave has no choice.
>   —Swahili proverb

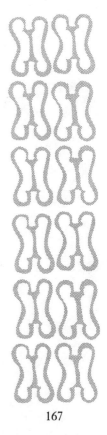

167

No more pleadin.
No more cryin.
Cuz I believe that I do hold up half the sky.

—recorded by Linda Tillery

Isn't it time we moved from myth to reality? Time we stopped allowing ourselves to be seduced into believing that silent suffering, bearing all burdens and being round-the-clock workers is something to be so proud of that we end up deifying—rather than moving to change—our condition?

—Marcia Ann Gillespie, writer and editor

You were born God's original. Try not to become someone's copy.

—Marian Wright Edelman

Now look here man
what you want me to do
Give you my stew meat
and credit you too?

—recorded by Bessie Jackson (Lucille Bogan), blues singer, from "Stew Meat Blues"

I totally and completely admit, with no qualms at all, my ego-mania, my selfishness, coupled with a really magnificent voice.
—Leontyne Price

I thought I'd go right ahead and take style to its limit. I want to be the last word. My philosophy is a belief in magic, good luck, self-confidence and pride.
—Grace Jones, vocalist and actress

You don't have to look poor, you know, you don't have to look down. For money is a medium of exchange, and that's all; but it is not a mind regulator unless you allow it to be.
—Charleszetta Waddles

Reclaiming that from which one has been disinherited is a good thing. Self possession in the full sense of that expression is the companion to self- knowledge.
—Patricia J. Williams

I am aggressive; I will not deny myself. I will not be one of those people talking about they need to get some training on how to be aggressive. To them, I say, all you have to do is come into a sense of yourself, announce that you are an African and intend to "be." That is some automatic aggression.

—Sonia Sanchez

Whoever wants me as I am is content.

—Ghanian proverb, Accra

Look-a here, look-a here, what you want me to do
Give you my jelly then die for you?

—recorded by Memphis Minnie, blues
singer, from "'Frisco Town"

Solitude, quality solitude, is an assertion of self-worth, because only in the stillness can we hear the truth of our own unique voices.

—Pearl Cleage

i can count the number of times i have viscerally wanted to attack deform n maim the language that i waz taught to hate myself in....

—Ntozake Shange

Mek youself flo' -clot(h), pipple wipe de(m) foot pa(n) you.

(If you) make yourself a floorcloth, people will wipe their feet on you.

—Creole proverb, British Honduras

I'm not living the blues; I'm just singing for the women who think they can't speak out. Can't a man alive mistreat *me*, 'cause I know who I am.

—Alberta Hunter, blues singer, age 87

You can stop honking that damned horn.
I don't pump no gas,
I don't wipe no windows or check no oil.
I'm not here to fuel your dreams.

—Patricia Smith from "No Gas"

And while life was often hard and resources scarce, we always knew who we were and that the measure of our worth was inside our heads and hearts and not outside in our possessions or on our backs.

—Marian Wright Edelman

No time to marry
no time to settle down
I'm a young woman
and ain't done running around
Some peole call me a hobo
some call me a bum
Nobody knows my name
nobody knows what I've done
I'm as good
as any woman in your town

—recorded by Bessie Smith from
"Young Woman's Blues", 1926

Take an honest assessment of what you do and do not like about yourself and evaluate how much of your feelings are based on white beauty standards or symbols of success. How often do you greet other black women you might pass on the street?…Have you ever considered that other black women might really value having you as a friend?

—Evelyn C. White

…We know it matters not what we have been
But this and always this: what we shall be.

—Angelina Weld Grimké, schoolteacher, writer, activist,
1880 - 1958, from "Then and Now"

I proudly love being a Negro woman. It is so involved and interesting.

—Anne Spencer, 1882 - 1975, poet

We do not need to be told what we should do or with whom we should identify in order to feel *good enough* about ourselves.

—Lena Wright Myers

No one can figure out your worth but you.

—Pearl Bailey

I told you one more lick
and this is it!
I'm going!

It's too late to apologize
Why should I believe your lies?
I'm going!...

Find somebody else to be beating on.
This one's gone.
You heard me right. I'm going, going, gone.

—Lorraine F. Joseph from "I'm Going"

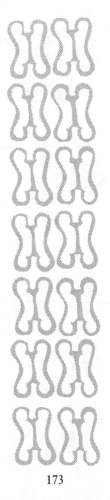

On reflection, one of the things I needed to learn was to allow myself to be loved.

—Isha McKenzie-Mavinga

And so what I've learned in the last 20 years is that *I* am the sole judge and jury about what my limits will be. And as I look toward the horizon of the next 20 years, it is *no…no* limit. With that kind of knowledge, I've grown as old as I can possibly be; the aging has stopped here, and now I just grow better.

—Gloria Naylor, novelist

Nigger nobility is reacting to oppression in a better way than you would if you were not oppressed. In other words, the worse you are treated the more noble you become…I think there is something very unwholesome about eating shit and calling it chocolate.

—Florynce Kennedy

Kye wazadde: tekiba kibi.

Whatever you have brought forth: is not bad.

—Luganda proverb

One of the greatest gifts of Black feminism to ourselves has been to make it a little easier simply to *be* Black and female. A Black feminist analysis has enabled us to understand that we are not hated and abused because there is something wrong with us, but our status and treatment is absolutely prescribed by the racist, misogynistic system under which we live.

—Barbara Smith

I got a lot
A lot of what I got.
And what I got is
all mine.

—sung by Ethel "Sweet Mama Stringbean" Waters

If you have no one to praise you, praise yourself.

—Grebo proverb, Liberia

You ran away
and left me on the shelf
Keep right on running
go chase yourself

—recorded by Daisy Martin, blues singer,
1923, from "What You Was You Used To Be"

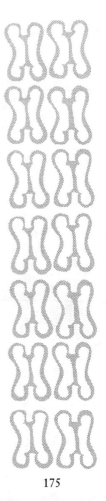

175

It is time for every one of us to roll up our sleeves and put ourselves at the top of our commitment list.

—Marian Wright Edelman

spoil me
wine and dine me
rub my feet
write me a poem
sing me a song
send me a dozen roses
embrace me
keep me warm and safe
open my door take my coat
surprise me on my job with a visit
call me just to say good-night
be with me
share with me
oh yeah go 'head spoil me
i will gladly return the favor
and let you meet
blackwoman

—Adele Sebastian from "Spoil Me"

To Our Sexuality

I may want love for an hour, then decide to make it two;
Takes an hour 'fore I get started,
maybe three before I'm through
I'm a one-hour mama, so no one-minute papa
ain't the kind of man for me!
> —recorded by Ida Cox, blues vocalist,
> from "One-Hour Mama"

I want to recognize a woman's right *not* to share or express her
sexuality and be able to do so without fear of reproach… It can
be a place of healing, of intense spiritual growth, of caring and
loving oneself sexually—whatever we need and want this space
to be, it can be.
> —Sabrina Sojourner

I answer: I want you like I want my coffee,
Honey Mama, hot and black,
I want you like I eat my greens—with my fingers and no fork,
like children want suckers
and like babies want tiddie.
> —SDiane Bogus from "How Does You Love Me,
> Sweet Baby?"

177

"ito ogodo" means
"to untie a woman's wrapper"

—Ibo

It is irrational that we are so uptight and so scared about morals that we would rather see little girls in the street pregnant than prevent that condition. It is a manifestation of our fundamental conflicts about sex.

—Faye Wattleton

If you don't like my sweet potato
what made you dig so deep
dig my potato field
3, 4 times a week

—recorded by Lil Johnson, blues singer,
from "You'll Never Miss Your Jelly"

By being sexually independent of men, lesbians, by their very existence, call into question society's definition of woman at its deepest level.

—Barbara Christian

In the face of a dominant culture that characterized all Black women as sexually promiscuous beings, public recognition of the self as a sexual being was seen as compromising the reputation of all Black women and of the race in general.

—Professor Hazel Carby, reclamation historian

call the name
and light the incense

i am going to burn

—Jodi Braxton from "Rising"

I can strut my pudding
spread my grease with ease
'cause I know my onions
that's why I always please

—recorded by Nellie Florence,
blueswoman, from "Jacksonville Blues"

My daughter spreads her legs
to find her vagina:
hairless, this mistaken
bit of nomenclature...
She demands to see mine...
my prodigious scallops
exposed to her neat cameo...
She is three; that makes this
innocent.

> —Rita Dove from "After Reading `Mickey in the
> Night Kitchen' For the Third Time Before Bed"

Oshu adi afu uya.

The genitalia (female) does not suffer disgrace.

> —Ibo proverb

It's so doggone good
till it make you bite your tongue
And I'm a coffee-grinding mama
won't you let me grind you some

> —recorded by Lucille Bogan, blues
> singer, from "Coffee Grindin' Blues," 1930

What the kids want to know is, what about lust? What do we do about it? And that's the very information that we don't want to give up. That is "our business." But they want to hear it from us, beacuse they trust us. And we have to struggle with how we do that: how do we share that information?

—Byllye Avery

If you got a good pussy
folks don't give it away
The rats may overtake you
need your pussy cat some day
—recorded by Jane Lucas from "Pussy Cat Blues," 1930

Anya huru ohu na achi ochi.

When the eye sees female genitalia it smiles.

—Ibo proverb

it ain't never smelt
like no fish to me
always smelled like
fresh chickens

—Elouise Loftin from "spoon say"

Each of us is entitled to define what our boundaries are and have them respected. Sex in and of itself is not wrong. What is done with sex can be very wrong.

—Sabrina Sojourner

I watched the fire for hours. It burned the way I burn when you slip a thick finger into me, when my voice breaks in my throat and my body pours hallelujahs into the cup of your hand.

—Patricia Smith from "Fire"

To Our Sisterhood

…being black and progressive doesn't mean you have left the scars of racism behind. If there is to be a sisterhood, not only must there be an examination of our history…but also how we deal with each other now.

—Jennifer Henderson, activist

If you speak, speak to her who understands you.

—proverb from Senegal

We resolve to be charitably watchful over each other; to advise, caution and admonish where we may judge there is occasion, and that it may be useful; and we promise not to resent, but kindly and thankfully receive such friendly advice or reproof from any one of our members.

—Article V, Constitution of the Colored Female Religious and Moral Society of Salem, Massachusetts, 1818

Think now
how to
reintegrate
ourselves
into our
Black woman
selves
and be
the bond
warp and weft
knit ourselves
together
in a
new
thot out unity
so we
don't
starve
to death....

—Sapphire from "Yellow"

All African-American women may not have rocking chairs, but
we have each other.

—Opal Palmer Adisa

Sorrow is like a precious treasure, shown only to friends.
                                        —proverb from Madagascar

I will not fight with you sister, anymore
For the road's too long and hard
And I need all my strength
To stay on it.
                    —Meiling Jin from "No More Fighting"

Sisters understand each other like no one else can. They need
each other. Sisters survive through each other, because when
the world keeps knocking them down they have each other to
fall back on.
                                        —Janet Singleton

Ageeteeraine nigo gaata eigufa.

United jaws crush the bone.
                    —Kigezi proverb, southwest Uganda

The black woman in jail seems to be too huge a dose of reality for the black woman outside. But for pure, unvarnished good luck, that would be her in prison: and what every black woman knows is that, if she slips up just a little, she can still end up there in 2 seconds flat. Under such circumstances, it is difficult for the black woman to feel sympathy for those sisters who didn't possess unearthly strength, who refused to play the game, who 'fucked up.'

—Michele Wallace

O, surely, round her place of rest
I will not let the weed be blest;
It is not meet that she should be
Forgotten or unblest by me.
—Ann Plato from "Reflections, Written On Visiting
The Grave of a Venerated Friend"

…Sisterhood is not an entitlement. Sisterhood is a gift. It is something that is developed, to be honored and respected.
—Rachel Bagby

…because we live in a patriarchy, we have allowed a premium to be placed on *male* suffering. Black women have also faced enormous hardship and pain, and rather than getting "behind" someone, we should be supportive of each other.

—from the National Black Feminist Organization "Statement of Purpose"

Tiyende pamodzi ndi mtima umo.

Let's go together with one aim.

—from a Nyanja song, Zambia

But you see now baby, whether you have a ph.d., d.d. or no d, we're in this bag together. And whether you are from Morehouse or Nohouse, we're still in this bag together.

—Fannie Lou Hamer, activist

Our skins may differ, but from thee we claim
A sister's privilege and a sister's name.

—Sarah L. Forten, poet, 1837

Bulala niko amani.

To be united is to be strong.

—Luyia saying

...we need to feel the cheer and inspiration of meeting each other, we need to gain the courage and fresh life that comes from the mingling of congenial souls, of those working for the same ends. Next, we need to talk over not only those things which are of vital importance to us as women, but also the things that are of especial interest to us as *colored* women.

—Josephine St. Pierre Ruffin (1842-1924), founded the New Era Club, which issued *The Women's Era* newspaper which she edited. This grew into the National Federation of Afro-American Women in 1895.

Words are easy, friendship hard.

—Ganda (Uganda) proverb

...you need friends like that. They have something you lack, like optimism. They make you feel everything is going to be all right with the world as long as they are around. It may seem a childish thing to be so dependent on friends. But is it really?

—Bessie Head

...African-American women may indeed find it easier than others to recognize connectedness as a primary way of knowing, simply because they are encouraged to do so by Black women's tradition of sisterhood.

—Patricia Hill Collins

And thus another strong and lasting thread
Is added to the woof our sex is weaving….

—Ada from "Lines"

A support group can help foster feelings of intimacy and trust between black women. For too long we have been told and perhaps too many of us believe that we will talk about each other, steal each other's men and stab each other in the back whenever we get the chance. These myths have lived long and destructive lives. It is time for black women to put them to rest, or at least to begin to talk about them openly.

—Evelyn C. White

Nyenga yobe mulunda.

A sister is a friend.

—Kaonde proverb

…being of one body yet sharing many voices is the daily life and strength of black women.

—Julia A. Boyd

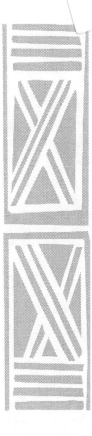

To Our Spirituality

...it is indispensable that every spiritual service, spiritual meditation and any devotion spiritually connected should be conducted with candle light.

—Mam'zelle Marie LaVeau

I am one African who needs and wants my God black,...preferably of the female gender.

—Bessie Head

The true believer begins with herself.

—Berber proverb

Blood has been used in traditions all over the world because it *is* the life force. We cannot live without it. But Nature in Her kindness and wisdom has provided woman with easy and regular access to this force, and all people receive life through the red flow of woman.

—Luisah Teish

…I betook myself to prayer and in every lonely place I found an altar.

> —Elizabeth, bondswoman and minister,
> born in Maryland, 1766.

Restore me, Adewoule.
Bring me to potions mixed
with whispers I barely remember…
Fortify ancestral memories to shore me
against this future.

> —Margaret D. Gill from "Bridge"

Spirit possession, that ecstatic moment of displacement central to the religious practices of Africans in the diaspora, literally embodies the transmission of cultural values across the Middle Passage.

> —Carolyn Cooper

When the winds of Orisha blow
even the roots of grass
quicken.

> —Audre Lorde from "The Winds of Orisha"

…there is no justification for demanding one uniform system of theology throughout the Christian community, but that theology reflects awareness of the horizon toward which all believers move.

—Mercy Amba Oduyoye

I cannot find a substitute word for all that is most holy but I have tried to deflect people's attention into offering to each other what they offer to an Unseen Being in the sky. When people are holy to each other, war will end, human suffering will end.

—Bessie Head

Go a cross-pass, you see ole 'ooman no trouble her.

(An old woman at the crossroads may be an obeah woman "setting" obeah for someone. Don't disturb her!)

—Jamaican proverb

Oshun is the Goddess of love, art, and sensuality. She is a temperamental coquette with much magic up her sleeve. She was the *me* I hid from the world.

—Luisah Teish

Okutaaga kwa rufu n'okuraguza.

Divining is to plead with death.
—Kigezi proverb, southwest Uganda

The idea that when people die their spirits go out I believe, but I believe that parts of the spirit that individuals need go to them…I believe that parts of people like John Garfield and Moms Mabley, the parts of them that I needed to be able to do what I'm doing, came into me. Parts of other people who are out in the world and who I don't know also entered into me. There's a very nice feeling that there are many, many spirits inside of me looking after me, along with my own sort of nuclei spirit….

—Whoopi Goldberg

To Our Survival

Nasarayaba.

I rise again.

—Garifuna, or Black Carib

If anyone should ask a Negro woman in America what has been her greatest achievement, her honest answer would be, "I survived!"

—Pauli Murray

Soa kenda hahay mitsako; soa lavo hahay mandeha.

Choking will teach you to chew properly; falling will teach you to walk properly.

—Malagasy proverb

'Mo yo lana', ko kan t'ebi.

'I was full yesterday' has nothing to do with today's hunger.

—Yoruba proverb

…who will deny that a little bit of luck and the proper mask did not also contribute to success?

—Jeanne Noble

Ah done been in sorrow's kitchen and ah licked de pots clean.

—Gulla proverb

A Negro woman has the same kind of problems as other women, but she can't take the same things for granted.

—Dorothy Height, president of the
National Council of Negro Women, 1963

It is precisely that Black women's history—from servitude and slavery to freedom—tells me how to live, how to survive, and how to be. To survive, Black women had to invent themselves and did. They defined the terms of their existence and much more.

—Erlene Stetson

Symbols communicate from one person's subconscious to the subconscious of another who shares the same identity and survival necessity.

—Dr. Frances Cress Welsing

Cross the river in a crowd and the crocodile won't eat you.
—proverb from Madagascar

You long to explode and hurt everything white; friendly;
unfriendly. But you know that you cannot live with a chip on
your shoulder even if you can manage a smile around your
eyes—without getting steely and brittle and losing the softness
that makes you a woman. For chips make you bend your body
to balance them. And once you bend, you lose your poise, your
balance, and the chip gets into you. The real you. You get hard.
—Marita Bonner

…I think, sometimes our madness is part of our survival.
—Maida S. Kemp

How I made it over
coming on over
all these years.
You know my soul looks back in wonder:
How did I make it over?

—sung by Mahalia Jackson

Ei ogiire niyo ekuha obugoga.

Get there, and you will then decide how to manage.
                                    —Kigezi proverb, southwest Uganda

I've come this far to freedom and I won't turn back.
I'm climbing to the highway from my old dirt track
        I'm coming and I'm going,
            And I'm stretching and I'm growing
And I'll reap what I've been sowing or my skin's not black.
                                    —Naomi Long Madgett from "Midway"

In order to survive, black women have become masters in the
art of being bicultural.

                                    —Julia A. Boyd

Manasa lamba manify: atao mafy, rovitra; atao malemy,
tsy afa-tseroka.

Like washing thin fabric: wash it hard and it will tear; wash it
gently and you will not get the dirt out.
                                    —Malagasy proverb

No matter what accomplishments you make, somebody helps you.
—Althea Gibson Darben, born 1927,
champion tennis player

Sikulu i ku hanya.

The great thing is to live.

—Tonga proverb

I have been *tired* for 46 years and my parents was *tired* before me and their parents were *tired*; and I have always wanted to do something that would help some of the things I would see going on among Negroes that I didn't like and I don't like now.
—Fannie Lou Hamer

Going slowly does not stop one from arriving.
—Fulfulde proverb

Giving up and "burnout" were not part of the language of my elders—you got up every morning and you did what you had to do and you got up every time you fell down and tried as many times as you had to to get it done right.
—Marian Wright Edelman

The blues helps us laugh at our misfortune, make light of our hazardous lives, and reaffirms that living is what life is about no matter how many hurdles we have to jump over.

—Opal Palmer Adisa

Black women as a group have never been fools. We couldn't afford to be.

—Barbara Smith

The black woman is independent. She's always been educated in the school of hard knocks.

—Dara Abubakari (Virginia E. Y. Collins)

Ani adi ahu obo gwu o ku.

The hot land does not burn (wither) obo gwu (a type of drought-resistant cactus).

—Ibo proverb

Mama may have
Papa may have
But God bless the child that's got his own
That's got his own.

—Billie Holiday, 1915 - 1959, blues singer and lyricist,
from "God Bless the Child," 1941

It is no longer a question of asking whether she is not too weak or too stupid to know how to pull a trigger or throw a hand grenade at the right moment, or hide something or other in the right place. A woman is just as capable of assimilating the techniques of guerrilla warfare as a man.

—Awa Thiam

Even those things that some include as "fiascos" have earned our admiration... Failures, maybe, but when you walk up to the plate swinging hard you don't hit a homer every time.

—Nannie Mitchell Turner, co-founder and publisher of the *St. Louis Argus*, 1912. "First Lady of the Negro Press and Dean of Newspaper Women"

...unless a woman learns not to be bitter about defeats and not to be arrogant about successes, each of them, both your success and your defeat can limit you.

—Maida S. Kemp

What will see me through the next 20 years (and I am less sure of those 20 than I was of "forever") is my knowledge that even in the face of the sweeping away of all that I assumed to be permanent, even when the universe made it quite clear to me that I was mistaken in my certainties, in my definitions, I did not break. The shattering of my sureties did not shatter me. Stability comes from inside, not outside....

—Lucille Clifton, poet and writer

The Yankees destroyed most everything we had...They didn't leave us a thing 'cept some big hominy and 2 banks of sweet potatoes. We chipped up some sweet potatoes and dried them in the sun, then we parched them and ground them up and that's all we had to use for coffee. It taste pretty good, too. For a good while, we just live on hominy and coffee.

—Fannie Griffin, ex-bondswoman, age 94
in the mid-1930's.

I didn't have anybody, really, no foundation in life, so I had to make my own way. Always. From the start. I had to go out in the world and become strong....

—Tina Turner

If there has been a secret to my success—a key ingredient or a personal philosophy—it is don't take no for an answer when you must hear yes.

—June Jackson Christmas, psychiatrist

Detention means...your seizure at dawn, dragged away from little children screaming and clinging to your skirt,...it means, as it was for me, being held in a single cell with the light burning 24 hours so that I lost track of time and was unable to tell whether it was day or night. Every single moment of your life is strictly regulated and supervised. Complete isolation from the outside world, no privacy, no visitor, lawyer or minister. It means no one to talk to each 24 hours, no knowledge of how long you will be imprisoned and why you are imprisoned, getting medical attention from the doctor only when you are seriously ill...Your company is your solitude, your blanket, your mat, your sanitary bucket, your mug and yourself.

—Winnie Mandela

Women understand the problems of the nation better than men for women have solved the problems of human life from embryo to birth and from birth to maturity. Women are the survival kit of the human race.

—Councillor Mandizvidza of Mucheke
Township, Zimbabwe, 1983

The most powerful weapon against African American women of all social levels is isolation.
—Chinosole, chair of the Women's Studies
Department of San Francisco State
University and member of African American
Advocates in Action for Children and Families

She could work miracles, she would make a
        garment from a square of cloth
in a span that defied time. Or feed twenty
        people on a stew made from
falleh-from-the-head cabbage leaves and a
        carrot and a cho-cho and a palmful
of meat.
—Lorna Goodison, Caribbean poet, from
"My Mother"

Biographical Statements

OPAL PALMER ADISA - mother, writer, storyteller, teacher.

CHRISTIA DANIELS ADAIR - b. 10/22/1893. Suffragette and civil rights leader. Politician for over 40 years in Texas.

TAIWO AJAI - born and raised in western region of Nigeria. First editor of African Woman, a journal started exclusively for women in 1975.

DR. ALPHA VERNELL ALEXANDER - b. Nashville, TN. Athletic Administrator/Sports psychologist.

IFI AMADIUME - Nigerian sociologist.

BYLLYE AVERY - founder and executive director of the National Black Women's Health Project in Atlanta, GA.

ALFREDA M. BARNETT - b. 9/3/04, daughter of Ida B. Wells- Barnett. Social worker and civic leader in Chicago.

RUTH NITA BARROW - b. 11/15/1916 in Barbados. Nursing educator.

FRANCES BEAL - active in Black Women's Liberation Committee of SNCC.

BERTICE BERRY - Ph.D., social commentator, comedienne.

MARY FRANCES BERRY - b. 2/17/1938, scholar, lawyer, educator, advocate. Member of US Commission on Civil Rights, 1980.

UNITA BLACKWELL - Mississippi's first Black woman mayor, elected in 1977.

JULIA A. BOYD - psychotherapist.

EARLENE BROWN - holder of American women's record in the shot put and discus, 1956, and 3-time Olympian.

ABENA BUSIA - poet and writer; associate professor of English as Rutgers University.

ANDREA R. CANAAN - writer and political activist.

SHIRLEY CAESAR - b. 10/13/1938, considered the Queen of gospel music. Grammy award winner.

ELIZABETH CATLETT - sculptor and lithographer.

LEAH CHASE - master chef in the Creole tradition.

VIOLET CHIDARARA - community leader, Zimbabwe, 1983

ALICE CHILDRESS - playwright.

MAY EDWARD CHINN, MD - b. 1896, d. 1980. Practiced medicine in NYC for over 50 years. For a long time, the only black woman MD in Harlem. First black woman to receive medical degree from Bellevue Hospital Medical College in 1922. Helped devise methods leading to early detection of cancer.

SHIRLEY CHISHOLM - b. 11/30/1924, first woman to actively run as presidential candidate and first black to seek the presidential nomination from a major party in 1972. First black woman elected US congressional representative in 1968.

LUCILLE CLIFTON - poet and writer.

JOHNETTA BETSCH COLE - b. 10/19/1936 in Jacksonville, FL. First Black woman president of Spelman College in Atlanta, GA.

CARDISS COLLINS - b. 9/24/1931, first woman to chair the Congressional Black Caucus in 1978.

JANET COLLINS - prima donna ballerina, was the first Black to perform on the stage of the Metropolitan Opera House in 1951.

MARVA COLLINS - b. 9/31/1936, educator, founded Westside Preparatory School, Chicago in 1975.

CAROLYN COOPER - professor and writer, scholar of literature at University of the West Indies, Mona, Jamaica.

FANNIE JACKSON COPPIN - Educator, mid-1800's.

JUANITA JEWEL CRAFT - b. 2/9/1902 in Round Rock, TX. Professional volunteer and activist in Dallas. At age 73, elected to seat on Dallas City Council.

SOR JUANA INES de la CRUZ - b. 1651, child prodigy, poet. Took the Holy Orders at Mexico City's Convent of St. Jerome.

MARIAN WRIGHT EDELMAN - b. 6/6/1939, first Black woman admitted to Mississippi Bar (1965); founded Children's Defense Fund (1973).

BUCHI EMECHETA - Writer, born in Lagos, Nigeria.

RUBY MIDDLETON FORSYTHE - teacher.

DR. ZELMA WATSON GEORGE - b. 12/8/1903 in Hearne, TX. Scholar, sociologist and social worker, musician. Member of the US Delegation to the General Assembly of the United Nations.

BERTHA KNOX GILKEY - activist for welfare and tenant rights.

JEWELLE GOMEZ - writer and activist.

MILDRED DENBY GREEN - was associate professor of music at LeMoyne - Owen College, Memphis, TN.

TINA SLOANE GREEN - Lacrosse and field hockey, U.S. Women's Lacrosse Team, 1968 - 1972.

ARDIE CLARK HALYARD - b. Covington, GA. Founder, with husband, of Columbia Savings and Loan Association, an organization chartered n 1924 to improve the housing situation for blacks in Milwaukee.

FANNIE LOU HAMER - was Vice-Chairman of the Mississippi Freedom Democratic Party (MFDP), and its candidate for Congress.

FRANCES E(LLEN) W(ATKINS) HARPER - born 1825, wrote one of the first recorded novels published by an African American women. This novel, *Iola Leroy or Shadows Uplifted*, was published in 1890.

JUANITA HARRISON - b. Mississippi. At age 36, worked her way around the world.

BESSIE HEAD - b. in Pietermaritzburg in 1937. South African-born novelist and story-writer, dies in exile in Serowe, Botswana, April 1986.

DOROTHY I. HEIGHT - b. 3/24/1912. For over 40 years, a staff member of the YWCA. President of National Council of Negro Women, 1963.

BEULAH SHEPARD HESTER - b. 10/7/1893, d. 1981. Social worker for over 30 years in Boston. First black appointed to Boston Board of Overseers of Public Welfare (1950 - 1961).

BELL HOOKS - writer and professor who speaks widely on issues of race, class and gender.

LENA HORNE - b. 6/30/1917. Dancer, singer; first black woman to sign with a major Hollywood film studio.

CLEMENTINE HUNTER - probably born in 12/1895 on Hidden Hill Plantation near Cloutierville, Louisiana. Primitive painter whose first public showing was in Louisiana in 1949. Known as the "Black Grandma Moses."

ZORA NEALE HURSTON - author of several cultural classics.

EVA JESSYE - b. 1895, credited with authenticating the sound of the first Broadway production of "Porgy and Bess."

CORA LEE JOHNSON - b. 1925 in GA. Activist.

BARBARA JORDAN - First Black woman elected to the state senate in Texas and first black woman from the South to be elected to Congress, November 1972.

JAMAICA KINCAID (Elaine Potter Richardson) - Novelist and fiction writer born in Antigua.

BISHOP LEONTINE KELLY - the second woman and first Black elected bishop in the United Methodist Church in 1984.

MAIDA SPRINGER KEMP - b. 5/12/1910 in the Republic of Panama. Trade union movement advocate and organizer in 1933 and many years afterwards.

CORETTA SCOTT KING - b. 4/27/1927, activist, musician, mother of 4.

EUNICE RIVERS LAURIE - b. 11/12/1899 in Early County, Georgia. Nurse.

ONNIE LEE LOGAN - b. 1910, 14th of 16 kids in Sweet Water, Marengo County, Alabama. Midwife.

AUDRE LORDE - b. 2/18/1934 in New York City. Poet, writer and activist.

ROZENA MAART - South African. One of 5 women founding WAR:
Women Against Repression, in 1986.

LINDIWE MABUZA - poet, scholar, activist. Chief representative of the African National Congress of South Africa to the U.S.

WINNIE MANDELA (Nomzamo Winifred Madikizela) - activist, b. 9/26/1936 in Pondoland, a "homeland" of South Africa.

JEWELL JACKSON MCCABE - president of National Coalition of 100 Black Women.

MINNIE "MEMPHIS MINNIE" DOUGLAS (McCOY)- b. June 24, 1902 in Algiers, Louisiana, died August 6 (?), 1973 in Memphis. Blues vocalist and composer.

ELLEN KATE CHOLOFELO NNOSENG MOTLALEPULE MERAFE - b. 1914 in Thaba Patchoa in the Orange Free State district of Thaba 'Nchu. Political activist in Johannesburg.

LUCY MILLER MITCHELL - b. in 1899 in Daytona Beach, Florida. Specialist in early childhood education; 50 years of activity and involvement nationally.

ELAINE MOHAMED - b. in England in 1961. Teacher at Saint Barnabas School in Johannesburg and executive member of the Progressive Teachers' Union.

RUTH MOMPATI - From Sierra Leone. Refugee from South Africa in political exile in Germany, 1982.

MELBA MOORE - b. 10/29/1948, performer and vocalist.

RUVIMBO MUJENI - Zimbabwe community development worker, 1983.

PAULI MURRAY - Civil rights lawyer and ordained priest of the Episcopal Church.

LAURETTA NGCOBO - b. 1932 in South Africa. Went into exile with 3 of her children in 1960. Writer.

CORNIA MZACA NKOMO - worker for a development organization in the rural areas of Zimbabwe, 1983.

SITHEMBISO NYONI - community development worker in Zimbabwe, 1983.

ELEANOR HOLMES NORTON - b. 1937. Equal rights activist.

ROSA PARKS - b. 2/4/1913 in Tuskegee, AL. Decided to test the practice of Jim Crow. Her action triggered the 1955 Montgomery bus boycott which lasted 381 days.

ETHEL PAYNE - b. 8/14/1911, journalist ands social change activist. War correspondent in Vietnam, 1966.

CARRIE SAXON PERRY - b. 1931 in Hartford, CT, the first Black woman to be elected mayor of a major U.S. city.

MARGARET PRESCOD-ROBERTS - born in Barbados. Co-founder of Black Women for Wages for Housework, U.S.A.

LEONTYNE PRICE - was the first Black to achieve world-wide status as "Prima Donna Assoluta". Has received 18 Grammy awards and the Presidential Medal of Freedom.

PHYLICIA RASHAD - b. 6/19/1949, actress.

BERNICE JOHNSON REAGON, Ph.D. - curator in the Division of Community Life at the Smithsonian Institution, National Museum of American History. Was member of the original SNCC Freedom Singers, founder of "Sweet Honey in the Rock," vocal ensemble.

ROPA RINOPFUKA - Zimbabwe educator, 1983.

JUDY SCALES-TRENT - associate Professor of Law and Jurisprudence, SUNY, Buffalo School of Law.

MARY ANN CAMBERTON SHADD (Cary) - b. 10/9/1823 in Wilmington, DE. First Black woman in North America to establish a weekly paper in mid-1800's, in Windsor, Canada.

ZODWA SIBANDA - founder member of WOZA: Women of Zimbabwe Association, borne out of concern for refugees, 1983.

ALTHEA T. L. SIMMONS - chief congressional lobbyist of the National Association for the Advancement of Colored People.

NONTSIKELELO ALBERTINA SISULU - Co-president of the United Democratic Front and leader in the organized anti-apartheid movement.

NORMA MERRICK SKLAREK - b. 4/15/1928 in New York City. First Black woman to become a licensed architect in New York and California.

BARBARA SMITH - co-founder and publisher of Kitchen Table: Women of Color Press.

BEVERLY SMITH - women's health activist and professional.

SABRINA SOJOURNER - individual and group development consultant, writer and lecturer living in Atlanta, GA.

SISTER SOULJAH (Lisa Williamson) - b. in the Bronx.

MURIEL SUTHERLAND SNOWDEN - b. 7/14/1916 in Orange, NJ. With husband, Otto, established Freedom House, a community institution in Roxbury, MA.

NORMA STEELE - b. in Jamaica. Social worker, mother of 2.

NIARA SUDARKASA - b. 8/14/1938, named president of Lincoln University, PA.

LUISAH TEISH - born and raised in New Orleans. Priestess of Oshun in the Yoruba Lucumi (African tradition).

MARY CHURCH TERRELL - b. 9/23/1863 in Memphis, TN; d. 7/24/1954. One of the earliest college educated American Black women. Activist; founded the National Association of Colored Women in 1896.

MARY CRUTCHFIELD THOMPSON - b. 11/30/1902 in Henderson, NC. One of the first Black women to graduate from the Tufts University Dental School, and the first to practice dentistry in the Boston area.

MIRIAM TLATI - b. 1933 in Doornfontein, Johannesburg. Novelist; the first Black woman to publish a novel in South Africa.

CHARLESZETTA CAMPBELL WADDLES - b. 10/7/1912 in St. Louis, MO. Founder and director of the Perpetual Mission for Saving Souls of All Nations, in Detroit. A "one-woman war on poverty," an ordained minister and mother of 10 children.

MICHELE WALLACE - cultural critic and writer.

MAXINE WATERS - b. 8/15/1938 in St. Louis, MO. Elected to the CA State Assembly, 1976. Considered the most influential woman in the Democratic Party.

FAYE WATTLETON - b. 7/8/1943, named president of Planned Parenthood Federation of America and first Black woman in the post, 1978.

FRANCES CRESS WELSING - Washington D.C. psychiatrist.

DOROTHY WEST - b. 6/2/1907 in Boston. An only child, completed her first short story at age 7. The only living writer of the Harlem Renaissance.

EVELYN C. WHITE - Writer. Former advocate for the Seattle City Attorney's Family Violence Project.

MARY LOU WILLIAMS (Mary Elfreida Scruggs-Burley) - b. 5/8/1910 in Atlanta. Pianist, composer and arranger, "The First Lady of Jazz."

MAXINE WILLIAMS - member of the New York City Young Socialist Alliance and the Third World Women's Alliance in 1970.

JULIA ZVOBGO - activist in pre-Independent Zimbabwe and exiled in 1983.

Acknowledgments

Grateful acknowledgment is given to the following copyright holders and publishers for granting permission to reprint extracts from material for this collection:

Sapphire for selections from *Meditations on the Rainbow*, P. O. Box 975, Manhattanville Station, New York, NY 10027, (c) 1987 by permission of the author.

Doris Davenport for selections from *Voodoo Chile /Slight Return: Poems*, Soque Street Press, P. O. Box 135, Cornelia, GA 30531-0135, (c) 1991 by permission of author.

Barbara Reynolds, editor, for excerpts from *And Still We Rise: Interviews with Fifty Black Role Models*, Washington, D.C.: USA Today Books, (c) 1988 by permission of editor.

Nancy Morejon for selections from *Where the Island Sleeps Like a Wing*, Oakland, CA: The Black Scholar Press, (c) 1985 by Nancy Morejon, by permission of the publisher.

Jayne Cortez for selections from *Poetic Magnetic*, Bola Press, P. O. Box 96, Village Station, New York, NY 10014, (c) 1987 by permission of author.

Thylias Moss for selections from *Hosiery Seams on a Bowlegged Woman*, Cleveland, OH: Cleveland State University Poetry Center, Cleveland State University, (c) 1983 by permission of author.

Michelle Cliff for excerpts from *Claiming an Identity They Taught Me to Despise* (reissued as *The Land of Look Behind*, Ithaca, NY: Firebrand Books), (c) 1985 by Michelle Cliff, by permission of publisher.

Luisah Teish for excerpts from *Jambalaya: The Natural Woman's Book of Personal Charms and Practical Rituals*, New York, NY: HarperCollins Publishers, (c) 1985 by Luisah Teish, by permission of publisher.

Ai for selections from *Fate*, New York, NY: Houghton Mifflin Company, (c) 1991 by Ai, by permission of publisher.

Lena Wright Myers for excerpts from *Black Women: Do They Cope Better?*, Englewood Cliffs, NJ: Prentice-Hall, Inc., (c) 1980 by permission of author.

Stephanie Byrd for selections from *A Distant Footstep on the Plain*, P. O. Box 516, Dryden, NY 13053, (c) 1981 by permission of author.

Linda Cousins for selections from *Black and in Brooklyn: Creators and Creations*, The Universal Black Writer Press, P. O. Box 5, Radio City Station, New York, NY 10101-0005, (c) 1983 by permission of editor.

Jeanne Noble for excerpts from *Beautiful, Also, are the Souls of My Black Sisters*, Englewood Cliffs, NJ: Simon and Schuster, (c) 1978 by Jeanne Noble, by permission of author.

Mary C. Lewis for excerpts from *Herstory: Black Female Rites of Passage*, Chicago, IL: African American Images, (c) 1988 by Mary C. Lewis, by permission of publisher.

Dorothy S. Redford for excerpts from *Somerset Homecoming: Recovering a Lost Heritage*, New York, NY: Doubleday, (c) 1988 by Dorothy S. Redford, by permission of publisher.

Emily Herring Wilson, editor, for excerpts from *Hope and Dignity*, Philadelphia, PA: Temple University Press, (c) 1983 by Temple University, by permission of publisher.

Naomi Sims for excerpts from *All About Success for the Black Woman*, New York, NY: Doubleday, (c) 1982 by Naomi Sims, by permission of publisher.

Annette Powell Williams for excerpts from "Dynamics Of A Black Audience" and Grace Sims Holt for excerpts from "Stylin' Outta The Black Pulpit" in *"Rappin' and Stylin' Out: Communication in Urban Black America*" edited by Thomas Kochman, Champagne, IL: University of Illinois Press, (c) 1972 by The Board of Trustees of the University of Illinois, by permission of publisher.

Willi Coleman for selections from *Home Girls: A Black Feminist Anthology*, Kitchen Table Women Of Color Press, P. O. Box 908, Latham, NY 12110, (c) 1983 by Willi Coleman, by permission of author and publisher.

Filomina Chioma Steady for excerpts from "African Feminism: A Worldwide Perspective," Rosalyn Terborg-Penn for excerpts from "African Feminism: A Theoretical Approach to the History of Women in the African Diaspora," Niara Sudarkasa for excerpts from "'The Status of Women' in Indigenous African Societies," and Martha K. Cobb for excerpts from "Images of Black Women in New World Literature: A Comparative Approach" in *Women in Africa and the African Diaspora* edited by Rosalyn Terborg-Penn, Sharon Harley and Andrea Benton Rushing, Washington, D. C.: Howard University Press, (c) 1987 by Rosalyn Terborg-Penn, Sharon Harley and Andrea Rushing, by permission of the publisher.

Rachel Bagby for excerpts from *Visionary Voices: Women On Power* edited by Penny Rosenwasser, Aunt Lute Books, 223 Mississippi, P. O. Box 410687, San Francisco, CA 94141, (c) 1992 by Penny Rosenwasser, by permission of publisher.

Anita Cornwell for excerpts from *Black Lesbian in White America*, Tallahassee, FL: The Naiad Press, Inc., (c) 1983 by Anita Cornwell, by permission of author and publisher.

Toni Morrison for excerpts from *Playing in the Dark*, Cambridge, MA: Harvard University Press, (c) 1992 by Toni Morrison, by permission of publisher.

Englewood Cliffs, NJ: Prentice-Hall, (c) 1969 by The Estate Of Lorraine Hansberry, by permission of publisher.

Nubia Kai for selections from *Solos*, Detroit, MI: Lotus Press, Inc., (1988) by Nubia Kai, by permission of publisher.

Angela Davis for selections from *Women, Culture and Politics*, New York, NY: Random House, Inc, (c) 1990 by Angela Davis, by permission of publisher.

Lois Johnson Clarke, editor, for selections from *Excerpts from the Journal of Annie Pace*, New York, NY: Vantage Press, (c) 1988 by Lois Johnson Clarke, by permission of editor.

Flo Kennedy for selections from *Color Me Flo: My Hard Life and Good Times*, Englewood Cliffs, NJ: Prentice Hall, Inc., (c) 1976 by Florynce R. Kennedy, by permission of publisher.

Leslie Reese for excerpts from *Upside Down Tapestry Mosaic History*, Detroit, MI: Broadside Press, (c) 1987 by Leslie Reese, by permission of publisher.

Wanda Coleman for excerpts from *Heavy Daughter Blues: Poems & Stories* 1968 - 1986, Santa Rosa, CA: Black Sparrow Press, (c) 1987 by Wanda Coleman, by permission of publisher.

Nikki Giovanni and Margaret Walker for selections from *A Poetic Equation: Conversations Between Nikki Giovanni and Margaret Walker* edited by Paula Giddings, Washington, D. C.: Howard University Press, (c) 1974 by Nikki Giovanni and Margaret Walker, by permission of publisher.

Daphne Williams Ntiri for selections from *One is Not a Woman, One Becomes: The African Woman in a Transitional Society*, Troy, MI: Bedford Publishers, Inc., (c) 1982 by Daphne Williams Ntiri, by permission of publisher.

Barbara Christian for excerpts from *Black Feminist Criticism*, New York, NY: Teachers College, Columbia University , (c) 1991 by permission of publisher.

June Jordan for selections from *Dry Victories*, New York, NY: Henry Holt and Company, Inc., (c) 1972 by June Jordan, by permission of publisher.

Tina Green, Dr. C. Oglesby, Alpha Alexander, and Mikki Franche, editors, for selections from *Black Women in Sport*, American Alliance for Health, Physical Education, Recreation and Dance, 1900 Association Drive, Reston, VA 22091, (c) 1981, by permission of publisher.

Aneb Kgositsile for excerpts from *Rainrituals*, Detroit, MI: Broadside Press, (c) 1989 by Aneb Kgositsile, by permission of publisher.

Nesha Z. Haniff, editor, for selections from *Blaze a Fire: Significant Contributions of Caribbean Women*, Sister Vision, Black Women and Women Of Colour Press, P. O. Box 217, Station E , Toronto, Ontario, Canada M6H 4E2, (c) 1988 by Sister Vision, Black Women and Women Of Colour Press in cooperation with Women and

Development Unit (WAND) Extramural Department, University of the West Indies, Barbados, by permission of the publisher.

Maxine Williams for excerpts from *Black Women's Liberation*, Pathfinder Press, 410 West Street, NY, (c) 1971, by permission of publisher.

Bessie Head for selections from *A Woman Alone*, Oxford, England: Heinemann Publishers, (c) 1990 by The Estate of Bessie Head, by permission of The Estate of Bessie Head.

Claudia Tate, editor, for excerpts from *Black Women Writers at Work*, New York, NY: Continuum Publishing Company, (c) 1983 by Claudia Tate, by permission of publisher.

Dr. Bertice Berry for excerpts from her performance at Michigan State University, East Lansing, MI on May 16, 1991, by permission of author.

Chinosole for excerpts from *Sojourner*, October 1992, by permission of Chinosole.

Jewelle Gomez for excerpts from *Hot Wire: The Journal of Women's Music and Culture*, May 1991, by permission of publisher.

Pinkie Gordon Lane for excerpts from *I Never Scream*, Detroit, MI: Lotus Press, (c) 1985 by Pinkie Gordon Lane, by permission of author.

Alice Walker for excerpts from *Hot Wire: The Journal of Women's Music and Culture*, January 1991, by permission of publisher.

Susheila Nasta, editor, for selections from *Motherlands: Black Women's Writing From, Africa,*
The Caribbean and South Asia, London, England: The Women's Press Limited, (c) 1991 by Susheila Nasta, by permission of the editor.

Karen Williams for excerpts from *Hot Wire: The Journal of Women's Music and Culture*, September 1991, by permission of publisher.

Becky Birtha for selections from *The Forbidden Poems*, Seattle, WA: The Seal Press, (c) 1991 by Becky Birtha, by permission of the publisher.

Brian Lanker, editor, for excerpts from *I Dream a World: Portraits of Black Women Who Changed America*, New York, NY: Stewart, Tabori & Chang, Inc., (c) 1989 by Brian Lanker, by permission of publisher.

Every reasonable effort has been made to trace the owners of copyright materials in this book, but in some instances this has proven impossible. The editor will be glad to receive information leading to more complete acknowledgments in subsequent printings of the book and in the meantime extends apologies for my omissions.